The Survival Guide for
Newly Qualified
Child and Family
Social Workers

of related interest

Good Practice in Safeguarding Children
Working Effectively in Child Protection
Edited by Liz Hughes and Hilary Owen
ISBN 978 1 84310 945 7

The Social Worker's Guide to Children and Families Law
Lynn Davis
ISBN 978 1 84310 653 1

See You in Court
A Social Worker's Guide to Presenting Evidence in Care Proceedings
Lynn Davis
ISBN 978 1 84310 547 3

The Child's World
The Comprehensive Guide to Assessing Children in Need
2nd edition
Edited by Jan Horwath
ISBN 978 1 84310 568 8

Handbook for Practice Learning in Social Work and Social Care
Knowledge and Theory
2nd edition
Edited by Joyce Lishman
ISBN 978 1 84310 186 4

The Post-Qualifying Handbook for Social Workers
Edited by Wade Tovey
ISBN 978 1 84310 428 5

Competence in Social Work Practice
A Practical Guide for Students and Professionals
2nd edition
Edited by Kieran O'Hagan
ISBN 978 1 84310 485 8

Learning Through Child Observation
2nd edition
Mary Fawcett
ISBN 978 1 84310 676 0

The Survival Guide for Newly Qualified Child and Family Social Workers

Hitting the Ground Running

Helen Donnellan and Gordon Jack

Jessica Kingsley Publishers
London and Philadelphia

First published in 2010
by Jessica Kingsley Publishers
116 Pentonville Road
London N1 9JB, UK
and
400 Market Street, Suite 400
Philadelphia, PA 19106, USA

www.jkp.com

Library of Congress Cataloging in Publication Data
Donnellan, Helen.
  The survival guide for newly qualified child and family social workers : hitting the
ground running / Helen Donnellan and Gordon Jack.
    p. cm.
  Includes bibliographical references and index.
  ISBN 978-1-84310-989-1 (pb : alk. paper) 1. Social work with children. 2. Family
social work. 3. Social service. I. Jack, Gordon. II. Title.
  HV713.D66 2010
  362.7--dc22
                                              2009020605

British Library Cataloguing in Publication Data
A CIP catalogue record for this book is available from the British Library

ISBN 978 1 84310 989 1

Printed and bound in Great Britain by
MPG Books Limited, Cornwall

Contents

Figures

Tables

Boxes

Acknowledgements

A small piece of evaluative research with newly qualified social workers and their managers, funded by the Peninsula Child Care Programme Partnership in 2006, provided the starting point for many of the ideas developed in this book. We are grateful to all of the participants who gave so freely of their time, as well as to the members of the Partnership Board for their interest and support, and to our research assistants, Tina Wilkinson and Jane Grose, for their help with the interviews.

Preface: The Background to this Book

In 2006/07, the first social work graduates began to emerge from new qualifying degree programmes, and the care councils in the four UK countries set about implementing new post-qualifying (PQ) frameworks for education and training. Against this background, the authors became interested in identifying the factors involved in social workers making the transition from qualification, through induction and consolidation, to established professionals. Our ideas prompted us to undertake a small-scale research study involving a total of 41 social workers, line managers and staff development officers from three statutory child care agencies in the south-west of England. The aim of the study was to investigate what newly qualified social workers know and do on entering first employment, and what links are made to ongoing professional development using the consolidation stage of the PQ framework in England. The findings from the study have informed much of our thinking in writing this book, and extracts from the questionnaires and interviews with those who took part appear regularly throughout the text, highlighting many of the key themes which emerged.

Introduction

A common experience for many newly qualified social workers is that they feel left very much to their own devices, making it up as they go along, sinking or swimming as the case may be. This book is intended to rectify that situation, helping you to successfully bridge the gap between qualification and established professional by providing a 'route map' to support and guide you through this transitional phase by:

- considering how knowledge and skills continue to be acquired and applied in the workplace as part of the development of professional practice and expertise

- discussing the duties and responsibilities you have as a social worker and how these are managed in organisations

- exploring ways of handling situations (with colleagues, managers and other professionals, as well as with service users) which may be new and challenging for you

- providing a range of strategies for managing yourself, your time and your workload

- offering suggestions for finding support, coping with stress and maintaining job satisfaction.

Each chapter includes a range of tasks, exercises and checklists, providing hints and tips to help you manage a range of different issues that are likely to arise during your first year as a newly qualified social worker (NQSW). These ideas are intended to trigger your thinking, to set you off in the right direction or to help you to avoid a particular difficulty. None provides a blueprint for success, and each is open to your own interpretation, for you to use, amend or discard, according to the particular circumstances you are dealing with at any particular time. We make no apologies for the fact that some of the advice included in the book may seem rather basic and self-evident, because it is often what is most obvious that actually becomes lost among all the competing pressures and demands of a new post.

Who is this book for?

As the book is intended as an introduction to social work for new entrants to the profession, it will be of interest not only to newly qualified social workers, but also to students in the final year of their qualifying programmes, the managers and supervisors of newly qualified social workers, and training and staff development personnel.

New entrants to the profession

This book aims primarily to provide advice and guidance for newly qualified social workers taking up their first post in work with children and families. It is designed to ease the transition from student social worker to qualified professional by providing the practical guidance and support needed in the first year or so in post.

Final year students

The impetus for this book came from the development of the new qualifying training programmes for social work and the implementation of the new post-qualifying frameworks for the profession across the UK. Qualifying students now spend a large percentage of their training time on placement in a variety of workplaces, and it is helpful for students to know right from the start how organisations operate and what to expect in looking ahead to their first employment. This book will provide a helpful overview of the rewards and pitfalls of the all-important transition from student to employee.

Managers and supervisors

Much of the advice and guidance in this book is based on the development of best practice in social work with children and families. An effective social worker will be one who recognises the benefits of ongoing learning and seeks out opportunities to reflect on their practice. This book therefore offers those who supervise and manage newly qualified staff an opportunity to reflect on a number of questions and key issues which typically arise for new entrants to the profession, evaluating the ideas and methods they currently use in order to improve their own practice.

Training and staff development personnel

Professional codes of practice lay a clear responsibility on organisations that employ qualified social workers to attend to their personal and professional development. This book could therefore be used as a reference book for trainers, mentors, supervisors, course leaders and others within the organisation who have a role in either supporting or developing newly qualified social workers. It could also help those in training and staff development units to make some of the links between qualifying programmes and their workplaces.

Although the current system for social work education, regulation and inspection reflects the devolved nature of governance of the four UK countries and incorporates local differences (see Table 12.2 in Chapter 12 for an outline), arrangements for the registration of newly qualified social workers are broadly similar so that, regardless of where in the UK you work, this book will provide equally relevant guidance and advice to support the initial professional development of NQSWs.

How is the book organised?

There are four parts in this book, arranged chronologically, which mark out progressive milestones along your route from the initial 'thud' of professional status as you hit the ground and keep running, warming to the task, jumping the hurdles and making your way safely to the finishing line at the end of your first year in practice, prepared for the next lap!

Each part contains three chapters gathering together topics relevant to that particular staging post. Some issues, for example orientation, are relevant at one specific point in time and are covered in depth in Part I. Others, such as supervision, coping and support, have been integrated into several chapters, to reflect your changing needs and thinking as you move through your welcome, induction and beyond. The four parts are described below.

Part I: *Thud!* Professional Status

Throughout Part I, we focus on the first few weeks of welcome, introduction and orientation to your first post as a qualified social worker, and aim to ease your transition into the workplace in these very early stages. The change from student to employee, the development of a professional orientation, and workplace motivators are primary considerations.

Part II: Warming Up

In Part II, we move on from early orientation to consider some of the priority issues which will present themselves during the next few months. Our focus now is on the more formal corporate and role-specific induction processes in your agency, with more about managing your time and planning your professional development.

Part III: Jumping the Hurdles

Part III focuses on the period after induction, as you take on an increasing workload and begin to deal with some of the stresses as well as the pleasures of the job. We explore ways of finding support from a wide range of sources, including a two-way 'supervisory alliance', as well as positive coping strategies for working in stressful situations.

Part IV: Going the Distance

As your day-to-day practice becomes more streamlined and you deal more confidently with the range of tasks allocated to you, Part IV considers the influence of the organisation on you and conversely how you can begin to have influence on the organisation. 'Going the Distance' also explores some of the frameworks for progression, promotion and professional development for the future.

How to use this book

You may like to read the book from cover to cover, methodically from front to back. Alternatively, you may prefer to dip in and out as the need arises, at times when you feel that you need particular information or support around a specific aspect of your role. We hope that it will be readily accessible to either approach.

However you decide to use it, you will find practical guidance and advice about how to approach the duties, roles and responsibilities you will be undertaking as a newly qualified social worker. The following list indicates some of the areas which are likely to be early priorities for you:

- managing the transition into the workplace and what is expected of me

- accountability and balancing care and control

- working within the agency policy and procedures

- coping with stress and finding support

- supervision

- personal and professional development.

Throughout the book a range of practice situations which are likely to arise are considered, and suggestions put forward which you could adopt or adapt to your own practice. None is 'writ in stone' nor offers the ideal blueprint for effective practice. The major part will depend on you, your own interpretation and how you are able to apply the ideas suggested.

Part I

Thud! Professional Status

Throughout Part I, we focus on the first few weeks of welcome, introduction and orientation to your first post as a qualified social worker and aim to ease your transition into the workplace in these very early stages.

The development of professional expertise and initial workplace motivators are primary considerations for Chapter 1 'Developing Professional Expertise'.

The change from student to employee in Chapter 2 'Transitional Change' includes consideration of the 'reality shock' which frequently accompanies the 'thud' of professional status. It is commonly acknowledged that change is rarely achieved without some stress and anxiety so our consideration of 'transitional change' includes some social strategies, coping mechanisms and sources of support, adequate for the first few weeks in your new post. However, given the importance of maintaining your motivation and building job satisfaction for your longer term survival, we return in depth to the negative consequences of stress, positive coping mechanisms, finding support and making best use of supervision in Part III 'Jumping the Hurdles'.

Preparations for Day 1 as well as a programme of basic introduction and orientation to your workplace are the main focus in Chapter 3 'Getting Started and What Helps'.

Part I concludes with a consideration in Chapter 3 of learning and reflection to anchor these two themes firmly at the very beginning of your professional development. You will see that they are woven throughout the text of the book and are revisited in different ways in Part II 'Warming Up' and Part IV 'Going the Distance', as you settle in and gradually take on a wider and more complex workload.

Chapter 1

Developing Professional Expertise

- Professional identity

- From novice to expert

- Continuing professional development

- Key considerations in developing as a professional

You will almost certainly have entered your new career with high expectations and motivation to become the best practitioner that you can. Your degree should have encouraged you to develop a commitment to ongoing enquiry and personal development, as well as equipping you with the skills to examine assumptions and use evidence to develop your own independent, critical judgements. These are the foundations of practice capable of meeting the challenges of complexity, uncertainty and unpredictability which characterise social work with children and families in the twenty-first century. But what is involved in moving forward from this point in your development towards becoming a fully established professional social worker?In attempting to answer this question, it is helpful, first of all, to consider what we mean when we talk about a profession, and related concepts such as professional expertise.

Professional identity

While professions can be defined in a number of different ways, most people would agree that they all involve claims to expertise, based on university-level specialist training, as well as official regulation. These characteristics mean that, to a greater or lesser extent, all professions exercise power and control, which promote positions of privilege, both socially and economically.

Issues of professional identity and concepts of the power derived from expertise have the potential to bring professionals into conflict, not only with one another, but also with those who use their services. However, the willingness of the social work profession to draw from a wide range of philosophies, ideas and methods, together with adherence to the principles of partnership working and anti-oppressive practice, have, to some extent, set it against the collective power associated with other professions. While consideration of these issues in relation to social work is therefore rather complicated, this should not prevent you from recognising in others, as well as aspiring to develop yourself, the sorts of knowledge and skills that give rise to legitimate claims of professional expertise. At the start of your professional career as a qualified social worker, it might be helpful for you to build up your own resource list of people who have particular areas of knowledge or expertise, including those in other agencies or professions, to whom you can turn for guidance and advice about specific aspects of your work (see Box 1.1).

Box 1.1 Defining an 'expert'

Can you think of someone who you regard as an 'expert' social worker? What contributes to your understanding of this person as an expert?

Here are some possible reasons for your judgement:

- Advanced theoretical or subject knowledge
- Many years of experience in a particular role or area of practice
- High level practice skills or analytical ability
- Valuable personal attributes

What are the motivators?

Personal motivation has an important role to play in developing your professional identity and expertise. As an extract from an interview with a newly qualified social worker shows, for example, if money is your only motivator then you are probably in the wrong job.

> **❝** The money is part of it. Of course it is. It's a job. But I wouldn't be doing it for the money I get paid if I didn't actually want to try and make a difference to people's lives, because I do. And that's the thing that holds me to the job, it's the people that I work with ... the variety ... the chance to try and make a difference, but recognising that the majority of the time, it's unlikely to. (Social worker, 12 months post-qualification) **❞**

The chance to 'make a difference' was among the reasons most frequently cited by the participants in our own study for choosing social work as a career, and we return to this issue a little later. Here, however, we are thinking about what will motivate and sustain you in the very early stages of your post-qualification employment.

Box 1.2 Assessing your professional motivation

Using the scale of 1–10 for each factor, choose the number which best describes your current level of satisfaction for each motivator:

Autonomy
I am developing skills and confidence to make my own critical judgements

| Not at all | 1 | 2 | 3 | 4 | 5 | 6 | 7 | 8 | 9 | 10 | Completely |

Challenge
I feel encouraged to take on new work and to try different approaches

| Not at all | 1 | 2 | 3 | 4 | 5 | 6 | 7 | 8 | 9 | 10 | Completely |

Support
I feel supported in my personal and professional development

| Not at all | 1 | 2 | 3 | 4 | 5 | 6 | 7 | 8 | 9 | 10 | Completely |

Acknowledgement
My role is clear and my work is recognised by the team and managers

| Not at all | 1 | 2 | 3 | 4 | 5 | 6 | 7 | 8 | 9 | 10 | Completely |

The exercise in Box 1.2 identifies four factors which are frequently quoted by professionals as primary workplace motivators for you to consider: autonomy, challenge, support and acknowledgement.

Low scores in all four areas indicate perceptions of limited autonomy, challenge, support and recognition, suggesting that your practice resembles that of a 'constrained conformist', operating in a directed and reactive way. In these circumstances you may consider your role to be one in which expectations are limited to 'doing what you are told' and 'toeing the party line'. Part of settling in to any new profession will involve an understandable and entirely reasonable preoccupation with how to get along in the system and get the job done. In the present context of public services in the UK, in which increasingly draconian political attitudes towards autonomy across the professions are evident, with power drawn away from individuals and towards central government, there is a tendency among many social workers to behave as constrained conformists. In what has become a very litigious society, organisations as well as individuals can struggle to maintain their independence, becoming risk averse to such an extent that autonomous professionalism is almost extinguished. The breaking down of professional skills into smaller, simpler activities, capable of allocation to non-professional support staff, has also eroded and effectively deskilled practitioners across the professions, from law and medicine to health and social care.

While all of this is undoubtedly true, the danger here lies in blaming others for the way that you practise social work, effectively allowing yourself to become a victim. It is therefore important to recognise that, whatever the external constraints under which you are practising, your own actions, attitude and approach to the job are also important. Consciously maintaining the stance of a 'proactive professional', with independent views based on your knowledge, skills and values, will influence not only the way you are perceived by others, including colleagues and other professionals, as well as people who use social work services, but also, perhaps more importantly, how you perceive yourself.

From novice to expert

The overwhelming majority of NQSWs are actively committed to keeping their knowledge up to date, and are enthusiastic about extending and enhancing their skills, as illustrated by two quotes from social workers.

> **"** Personally, I like going on courses. I want to learn, I don't want to get rusty, so I will put myself on courses. (Social worker)
>
> And I really value training. I've always done a lot of training in my time in social care, because there's a lot more that I don't know than I do know and any bit that I can find out is useful to me. (Social worker) **"**

It is likely that your degree will have encouraged a commitment to ongoing enquiry, examining assumptions – those of others as well as your own – and to questioning, analysing and arguing from evidence to develop your own independent critical judgements. These skills provide the foundations for the development of your own professional 'expertise'; but what processes are involved in translating the skills and knowledge that you have acquired from your training into professional expertise?

Knowing what and knowing how

Based on a study of adult learners drawn from a wide range of professions in which, like social workers, individual practitioners were required to deal with problems arising in unstructured and unpredictable situations, Dreyfus and Dreyfus (1986) divided the knowledge and skills required to develop professional expertise into two types:

- Knowledge based on facts and rules – in which practitioners can say that they *know what*. You might think about this as technical knowledge.

- Knowledge derived from practice experience – in which practitioners demonstrate that they *know how*. You might think about this as practical knowledge or skills.

Table 1.1 Stages of skills acquisition

Skill level	Types of rules for decision-making	Exercising judgement and prioritising information	Process of decision-making	Level of responsibility and involvement in the situation
1. Novice	Context free	None	Analytical	Detached
2. Advanced beginner	Context free and situational	None	Analytical	Detached
3. Competent	Context free and situational	Chosen deliberation	Analytical	Detached understanding and deciding but involved in outcome
4. Proficient	Context free and situational	Experienced	Analytical	Involved understanding and detached deciding
5. Expert	Context free and situational	Experienced	Intuitive	Involved

Source: Dreyfus and Dreyfus (1986)

Dreyfus and Dreyfus then went on to propose a staged model of the development of professional expertise, with five levels of skill, each consisting of four elements, as set out in Table 1.1.

Context-free rules are those founded on the technical aspects (know what) of knowledge, in which you learn to recognise a range of objective facts and features which are relevant regardless of context. As a 'novice' learner at the start of your social work training, you are likely to have formulated a number of context-free rules, based on your personal biography and values, and the methods and theories that you were first taught. Then, progressing through Stages 2 and 3 as an 'advanced beginner' and a 'competent' practitioner, you are likely to have gradually begun to modify and adapt these rules in the light of your experiences in different situations, initially in practice learning settings, and more recently in the workplace. During these stages of development, some of your early, context-free rules may be jettisoned altogether, but those that are retained will be gradually amended, modified and adapted to become 'situational rules', founded on the second type of knowledge, identified earlier as 'know how', or practical knowledge.

There comes a point in this natural progression when the sheer number of 'rules' becomes overwhelming so that, at the 'competent' practitioner stage, which is probably where you are in your professional development at the present time, you begin to develop a hierarchical process of decision-making, ordering and prioritising particular elements and selecting an action plan based on conscious decision-making processes. This is when you begin to realise that your job performance is becoming more streamlined. Later on, at the 'proficient' practitioner level, the process of conscious choice and deliberation begins to be replaced by a greater reliance on understanding and recognition of similar situations and patterns from previous experiences, but even at this stage you are still likely to be thinking in a more or less deliberate and analytical way about exactly what to do. It is only, finally, at the 'expert' stage that all aspects of professional thinking and doing become fully integrated and more or less intuitive.

Taking these ideas a step further, Fook *et al.* 2000 undertook a study in Australia which tracked the professional development of social workers for a period of five years, from the beginning of their training through to the workplace as qualified employees. This study enabled them to construct a theory of the development of professional expertise, in which they identified movement across 11 dimensions including knowledge, skills, values, context, reflexivity, flexibility and creativity, use of theory, and perspectives on professional identity. The progression suggested by Fook *et al.*, from novice to expert practitioner, is summarised in Table 1.2.

Together, these models provide a useful framework for mapping the changes in your thinking which are likely to occur over time, as you take on more complex work, applying your own situational rules while also developing and understanding the processes for prioritising and organising plans for action, and recognising and using the repeating patterns in your own experiences which finally become intuitive responses. The important point is that these changes are liable to occur at different rates and at different times, and not necessarily in a linear fashion. In fact, while the majority of practitioners will become 'proficient', reaching Stage 4 in the Dreyfus and Dreyfus (1986) model, not all will necessarily reach Stage 5 – that of the 'expert'.

In these early stages of your career, you may well feel that all of this is still a long way off. At the moment, you are more realistically

Table 1.2 Expertise development

From novice		To expert
Using context-free rules	→	Applying and developing own range of situational rules, with the ability to select and prioritise, using independent critical judgement; generating a range of options; recognising multiple viewpoints
Dealing with personal and professional tensions; often a 'constrained conformist', concerned with interpreting legislation and its influence on job performance; vision limited to 'how to get along in the system and get the job done'	→	Demonstrating broader values and commitment to the profession; using the ability to frame change as a challenge or opportunity; separating personal and professional; grounded yet transcendent
Knowledge and skills seen as domain specific and focused on the individuals in a situation	→	Knowledge used creatively and readily transferred across contexts; planning and action undertaken as a holistic exercise
Passive detachment; standing outside the decision-making process but beginning involvement in outcomes	→	Acting reflexively; interested in both process and outcome
Outcome oriented	→	Process oriented; risk-taking, creative and flexible
Drawing on pre-professional personal experiences	→	Using an amalgam of knowledge to create own theory or knowledge, which is transferable and can be generalised across situations

Source: adapted from SCWRU (2008)

engaged in handling the transition from student to qualified professional in a new workplace, and this is where the arrangements for NQSWs within your employing organisation play an important role in your development.

An apprenticeship model

For some employers and professional bodies, the post-qualification development of social workers is understood primarily as a technical apprenticeship, with new workers being inducted into a prescribed body of knowledge and skills in which they are required to become proficient. This model, exemplified by the programme developed by the Children's Workforce Development Council (CWDC) for NQSWs (CWDC 2008a), typically involves a new entrant to the profession being supervised by a senior colleague charged with responsibility for ensuring that a clearly defined set of knowledge and skills is passed on. The notion of an apprenticeship also carries with it elements of organisational control, to ensure ongoing procedural correctness in the ways in which the knowledge and skills transmitted are taken up and used (Tickle 1994, p.39). An apprenticeship is deemed to have been successfully completed once the new entrant to the profession has become technically proficient, having been assessed as such against a set of standard performance criteria.

Besides the one-to-one supervision relationship, organisations or teams adopting the apprenticeship model might also provide you with additional learning opportunities during your first year in employment, including:

- shadowing a qualified member of staff for an agreed period of time, across the range of duties applicable to your particular work setting

- observing a specific piece of agency process or procedure, for example a child protection or family group conference

- joint working, without case responsibility, alongside an experienced practitioner in an area or context which is new to you, for example court work or adoption.

Unfortunately, in the present context of staff shortages in children's social services, frontline workers are unlikely to be offered opportunities like this for a prolonged period of time, if at all. However, these sorts of experiences can provide very helpful learning in the early stages of your post-qualification employment. So, if they are not offered to you as part of your induction, it is worthwhile asking your supervisor if they can be provided, or exploring with your colleagues whether they can be arranged on a more informal basis.

Continuing professional development

It is important to recognise, however, that some significant limitations arise if we restrict our understanding of professional development to the enhancement of technical skills and knowledge within an apprenticeship model. It will be clear from what has been said already that this model is best suited to meeting the need for the development of technical skills and knowledge applied in contexts which are well established and relatively stable. This means that it is often inadequate, on its own, for meeting the professional development needs of social workers operating in the rapidly changing, complex and uncertain contexts within which they typically work. What is called for, therefore, is a more holistic model of continuing professional development (CPD) that is capable not only of transmitting the skills and knowledge needed in the past, but also of responding to the changing contexts of professional practice in the future. The main focus of this approach is the provision of opportunities for social workers (and their managers) to reflect critically upon their experiences in the workplace in a way that helps them to both learn from what they have already experienced, and to transfer that learning intelligently and imaginatively to new situations.

In the past it was possible (and even largely acceptable) simply to qualify as a social worker and then to get on with the job, without any requirement to demonstrate further professional development, as illustrated in the quotation from an established social work practitioner.

> **"** I know I had four or five years' ducking and diving, avoiding our training officer who said you must get this PQ. (Social worker) **"**

However, with the advent of professional registration and post-qualifying education and training, there is now a formally recognised need for social workers, like other professionals, to continue to develop their learning throughout their careers, with formal requirements for post-registration training and learning (PRTL) specified by the regulatory bodies for the profession. There will be more to say about CPD (and PRTL) in Chapter 12.

Key considerations in developing as a professional

- While recognising the external constraints under which you may be practising, understanding what motivates you as a social worker should help you to consciously maintain the stance of a proactive professional, developing independent views based on your own knowledge, skills and values.

- There are limitations to an apprenticeship model of induction, focusing solely on technical proficiency and procedural correctness. Ongoing learning and the accumulation of 'practice wisdom' must be sustained as central elements of your professional development.

- Throughout your career you will need to use and develop skills in questioning, debating, analysing and arguing from evidence, as part of your developing professional expertise.

- Take responsibility for your own continuing professional development from day one. It is important to recognise that learning comes through doing, and that 'not knowing' is a necessary part of the process for everyone. Make full use of your status as a newly qualified social worker to ask for help, guidance and advice when you need it.

Chapter 2

Transitional Change

- The transition gap
- Reality shock
- Key considerations in bridging the transition gap

For most practitioners, the 'thud' of professional status heralds a sometimes bewildering period of change, with adjustments needed to come to terms with the tensions between their initial expectations and the harsh realities of social work practice in the 'real world'. In this chapter, we consider the processes involved in making the shift from student to employee, identifying and exploring a 'transition gap' through which all NQSWs in the early stages of their professional development must pass, almost as a 'rite of passage'.

The transition from student to employee is likely to be one of the most challenging periods of change that you will ever be required to negotiate. The success of your 'socialisation' into the profession depends, among other factors, on your ability to maintain the perspectives which you brought with you to your first job, at the same time as adapting to the cultures and traditions that you find there.

The transition gap

Despite the evidence of well-established theories about the process of developing professional expertise discussed in Chapter 1, the transition from social work student to qualified professional during the first 12 months in employment is just beginning to be recognised as a specific phase of development in social work. In contrast to other professions involved in the delivery of children's services, such as teaching and nursing, little attention has been given to trying to describe or explain the processes involved in making this transition successful, with beginning practitioners largely being left to their own devices to cope with this period of change. However, while there are important differences in the contexts and perspectives of the various professional groups involved in the children's services workforce, almost without exception they are united in feeling that their first period in employment as qualified practitioners represents 'a testing time', and one in which 'feeling unprepared is almost inevitable'. Our own interviews with NQSWs revealed powerful feelings likened to being 'thrown in at the deep end' before you had been taught how to swim, and we became acutely aware of the existence of a significant but largely unacknowledged 'gap' between the expectations and experiences of students on their final placements, and the reality of practice in their first 12 months of post-qualification employment. Recognising the existence of a gap is the first positive stage in addressing the deficit and getting the help and support that you might need.

Moving from student to employee

So what are the key differences that define the 'gap' between being a student and a qualified employee? One newly qualified social worker expressed his feelings as follows.

> **"** Ultimately, as a student, you're not responsible ... when you come back here qualified you're given a caseload, and that's the difference, you are responsible and the buck stops with you and that leaves a different feeling inside. (NQSW) **"**

In leaving behind student status, you will no longer:

- be answerable to the academic world of your tutors, teachers or the university

- have the ready support of a group of students, all facing similar problems together

- be finishing your placement in a few weeks.

In taking on qualified social worker status you will:

- have duties and responsibilities defined by the policies and procedures of your employer

- carry a corporate identity

- be carrying full case responsibility

- be personally accountable for your decisions and actions.

Taken together, these changes will doubtless create pressure on you to perform confidently and well, and the 'gap' between your previously familiar student role and your new identity may well come into sharp focus. The world of science explains the phenomenon of change from one state to another through the laws of thermodynamics, in which transitions between the three states of matter – solid, liquid and gas – typically involve large amounts of energy. However, this energy is described as 'latent', meaning that it is normally hidden from view, much as it appears to be in the crucible of first employment, when practitioners attempt to make the transition from one state (student) to the next (qualified employee). At the present time, the energy involved in successfully making the leap across this transition gap is either hidden or completely unrecognised.

Underpinning and overarching knowledge

The transition gap is characterised by the interaction between two different sorts of knowledge – 'overarching' and 'underpinning'. The first is derived largely from your degree course, while the second mainly develops in your practice learning and employment settings (Nellis 2001). Both are essential to the development of competent professional practice, and bringing them together into an individually balanced equilibrium is one of the main tasks for a successful transition into the profession. We have taken these ideas a little further and represent the two strands of developing professional practice in Figure 2.1.

The specific contribution of 'overarching' knowledge is the 'graduateness' which, as a successful student, you will bring with you into the workplace. As well as subject-specific knowledge, 'graduateness' incorporates the ability to take a wider view, to contemplate ideas, to tackle complexity, to separate fact from opinion, to analyse and draw

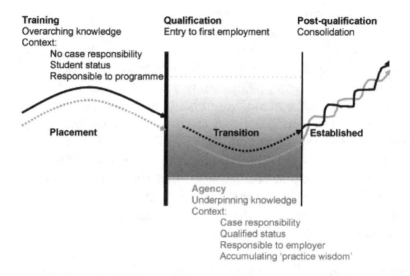

Training
Overarching knowledge
Context:
    No case responsibility
    Student status
    Responsible to programme

    Placement

Qualification
Entry to first employment

Transition

Post-qualification
Consolidation

Established

Agency
Underpinning knowledge
Context:
    Case responsibility
    Qualified status
    Responsible to employer
    Accumulating 'practice wisdom'

Figure 2.1 The transition 'gap'

reasoned conclusions, and perhaps above all to foster an inquiring and independent mind. The black line in Figure 2.1 represents this university-related strand of knowledge, and we have represented it as a solid line during training in recognition of its dominance at this stage. It provides you with the subject-specific knowledge from which you will have begun to develop, among other things, your initial repertoire of context-free rules, which we considered earlier, as part of the decision-making processes which are tested and explored in your practice placements. At the same time, 'underpinning' knowledge, in and of the agencies in which you are on placement, is also developing. However, while you are a student, without full case responsibility and with close links to the university, the development of underpinning knowledge is more limited, so it has been represented by a dotted grey line in Figure 2.1.

The 'thud' with which qualified status arrives is denoted both by the thickness of the first vertical black line, and also the gap which follows in the development of both types of knowledge in the very early stages of transition into first employment. This is swiftly followed during the transition period by a switch in emphasis from the original dominance of overarching knowledge, now shown as a dotted black line, to prioritising the acquisition of underpinning knowledge within your employing agency, represented as a bold grey line. Now the context for the development of your learning is that you hold qualified status and full case responsibility, with your original ties to the university replaced by obligations to your employers.

It is only after the transition gap has been successfully traversed, and you begin to consolidate your practice as an established professional, that learning along both of these dimensions becomes more balanced and integrated. This is probably the point at which you will feel willing and able to take on more formal post-qualifying (PQ) studies, and will be looking to the professional framework to support your development through the next (consolidation) phase. There is more about the PQ framework in Chapter 12.

You will no doubt have noticed that these ideas resonate with the theories put forward by both Dreyfus and Dreyfus (1986) and Fook *et al.* (2000) discussed in Chapter 1. All of this evidence points to the realisation common to all new entrants to any profession that 'learning comes through doing'. The result is that, however well prepared you might feel as you begin your first employment, the 'underpinning' knowledge that is necessary for competent professional practice cannot be provided in advance of taking the plunge, and can be properly integrated with 'overarching' knowledge only over a significant period of time. These theories and ideas of expertise and professionalism lead us inexorably to the recognition of a period of transitional change in the first year in employment, which is initially characterised by a 'gap' through which all newly qualified social workers must pass before they can become established professionals.

Induction or probation?

It is also worth pointing out here that, although specific programmes for newly qualified social workers, such as the pilots introduced by the Children's Workforce Development Council in England in 2008 (CWDC 2008a), may make a contribution to bridging the 'transition gap', they currently draw heavily on an apprenticeship approach to induction, with little attention given to the processes of *learning*. Practitioners are effectively viewed as technicians, acquiring the knowledge and skills deemed necessary to 'do the job', the demonstration of which is monitored and assessed with a view to confirming appointment. While all of this is important, if you want your learning to be sustained as a central element of your continuing professional development, it is essential that you find sources of mentoring as well as monitoring, and personal advice and support as well as assessment. These are issues to which we return in more detail in Part IV of this book.

Reality shock

As we have already noted, a bewildering level of change frequently accompanies the 'thud' of professional status. As far back as 1974 Kramer introduced the term 'reality shock' to characterise the adjustments needed as students came to the realisation that there was indeed a gap between their professional expectations and the harsh realities of the 'real world'. In Kramer's (1974) case it was nurses, but the shock is experienced to no lesser extent by new entrants to the social work profession, and the tensions between ideal and real practice begin to manifest themselves almost immediately, as reflected in the following extracts from newly qualified social workers.

Working to deadlines

The pressure from your line manager is more likely to be for the completion of reports according to a particular timescale, rather than the high quality piece of considered writing that you will have been encouraged to produce for assessment as a student.

> Because I make time for report writing, other things have to go. I'm not going to hand in a poor quality piece of work … I'm not prepared to do that. (NQSW)
>
> It isn't as though I haven't done the work, the work has been done, I just haven't got the time to write it all up every day. (NQSW)

Individual accountability

Your primary focus in a case may be on caring for service users, but you will often be required to balance this with aspects of control, in which you have to take responsibility for unpopular decisions from the service users' perspective, and you will be disliked as a result.

> **❝** It hasn't been easy over the last six months and I've realised what people, like, they really do hate you as well. You turn up and there's no way of sugar-coating what you've got to say and to work with people that absolutely detest the ground I walk on has been a real experience. (NQSW) **❞**

Working within agency policy and procedures

Sometimes, you may go through the whole assessment process and come to a decision which is not then supported by your manager or the agency in quite the way you had expected.

> **❝** I'm struggling with it at the moment if I'm honest. The reasons I came into social work are still very much there in my value base. I'm finding it conflicts with the position of the local authority. You know, I've got a case at the moment … I know the decision is about long-term budgeting, so it's kind of frustrating really that you are constrained by policy rather than good practice. (NQSW) **❞**

These tensions really stem from differences between the expectations you have of yourself, your concept of the value-base of the profession, and your day-to-day experiences of work situations where budget management, performance targets and deadlines all take on a greater significance. This is a hard nut to crack, but those who are able to successfully manage the duality of their role will have developed the ability to balance their personal involvement in people's lives with the ability to stand back, make judgements and reach often hard decisions. Referring back to the model of expertise development discussed in Chapter 1, these abilities generally appear among the criteria attributed to 'expert' status, including such things as 'ability to prioritise, use independent critical judgement, recognise multiple viewpoints, separate personal and professional, and apply a process orientation'. While they are unlikely, therefore, to be fully developed in the first 12 months after qualification, an awareness of the developmental nature of these aspects should help you to frame your feelings positively, as part of the initial process of your socialisation into the social work profession.

Change and social strategies

Each one of the changes accompanying your transfer from qualifying training into the workplace needs careful attention if you are to manage the process successfully. Social work is a complex and difficult job, and you should not expect the first 12 months to be plain sailing. The ease with which you are able to move through the initial weeks in post, making adjustments and settling in to the workplace, will depend on a number of factors related to your own abilities, situation and circumstances, as well as what the organisation has to offer by way of support. We have represented these processes of change, from one overlapping state to another, as you become socialised and established in the workplace, in Figure 2.2.

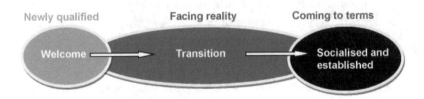

Figure 2.2 Professional socialisation

For some, transition is primarily a pragmatic step which can be taken at an early stage, exemplified by a comment from a newly qualified social worker.

> **"** Since it's not making me jump up and down any more, I guess I've grown up. I'm just going to work with what I have, keep a lid on and roll with it really. (Social worker, 12 months post-qualification) **"**

Others may take longer, and look for more support in coming to terms with the changes that will be needed to help them feel at ease within the agency. As we noted at the beginning of this chapter, the process of 'socialisation' will be strongly affected by the character, ethos and belief systems of others in your team and within the wider organisation. However, you do not have to consider professional socialisation as a *fait accompli*, in which you have no part and in which the organisation necessarily holds sway. It is better treated as a process of negotiation, in which individuals not only adjust to, but also can influence, the requirements and demands of the workplace. One useful model (Lacey 1977) suggests that there are three different strategies in this process, broadly described as follows:

- *Strategic compliance*: where, finding yourself in a culture which does not accord with your own values and beliefs, you simply comply with requirements which you may well feel are imposed upon you. This approach allows you to 'get along in the system', but does little to ease your integration into the team. Strategic compliance is most likely to be experienced in the very early stages of employment, as you first encounter some of the tensions between personal and professional expectations.

- *Internalised adjustment*: which occurs when you find that you are in sympathy with the expectations and values of at least some of the members of your team or unit within the agency. Taking as many opportunities as possible to talk with and work alongside peers and colleagues will be very helpful to you in seeking out the 'kindred spirits' that will help you to feel at ease within the organisation. The newly qualified social worker quoted above seems to have reached this stage of internalised adjustment after some 12 months in post.

- *Strategic redefinition*: in which you may attempt to introduce some new and creative elements into the workplace. The success or otherwise of this strategy will depend to a large extent on the ethos of the agency and its ability and willingness to respond to the changes proposed.

Adopting any one of these strategies, at an appropriate time, should help you to make sense of some of your emotional responses to the tensions between ideal and real practice, and how you are feeling about yourself, your colleagues and your agency, but other coping mechanisms will also be needed as you negotiate your way into the profession and your new workplace.

Coping

Coping is the means by which you maintain a sense of personal ac-complishment and job satisfaction. Part III focuses in detail on coping mechanisms, finding support and getting the most out of supervision, but coping is also part of the repertoire of skills that you will need when traversing the transition gap, and so one or two mechanisms are given an early mention here.

There is evidence (Stalker *et al.* 2007) that where those in caring professions are able to employ active, engaged coping mechanisms, they are more likely to maintain their sense of personal accomplish-ment, even though they might also be experiencing considerable stresses. By contrast, using disengaged strategies has a negative effect on levels of satisfaction, and it is in this state that people may well resort to 'going off sick' as the only solution to the stress and emo-tional exhaustion they are experiencing. Examples of both engaged and disengaged coping mechanisms are listed in Table 2.1.

Table 2.1 Coping mechanisms

Engaged	Disengaged
Problem-solving	Problem avoidance
Seeking social support	Social withdrawal
Expression of emotions	Wishful thinking
	Self-criticism

Your passage through the overlapping phases of professional socialisa-tion (Figure 2.2 above) will be most effectively managed where you are able to make full use of a range of engaged mechanisms.

In your own experiences of coping with difficult, challenging or stressful situations, either in one of your practice learning placements on your social work degree programme or in a previous job, what strategies and approaches have you called on to address the problems you faced? See Box 2.1.

Box 2.1 Reflecting on your own experiences

Think of a situation in which your own coping mechanisms have been tested.

- Which, if any, of the criteria listed in Table 2.1 (engaged or disengaged) did you employ?

- How well did you cope?

- In what ways might you change your approach next time?

The principal message here is that no one resource is likely to meet all of your needs and although some formal arrangements will be in place as part of your job description, for example supervision, you will need to be proactive and creative in seeking out and making use of a wider range of sources of help and support at different times, according to your own needs. These may include the following:

- making positive use of formal supervision

- seeking advice from your buddy or mentor

- calling on informal networks with colleagues and peers

- making use of family and friends

- emailing other newly qualified students from your course

- enquiring about links with other newly qualified staff in the same building, team or locality, either for individual contact or to get together as a group

- finding out about any other support arrangements which are part of your probationary year.

Part III takes up in detail the issues of supervision, support and the role of managers in recognising transitional change and meeting the emotional needs of newly qualified staff.

Key considerations in bridging the transition gap

- Learning comes through doing, in which time is needed to build experiences in a range of situations.

- However well prepared by training, the underpinning knowledge required in first employment cannot be provided in advance of 'taking the plunge'.

- The first year must be more than an apprenticeship with a clear focus on mentoring rather than monitoring, advising rather than assessing, and supporting rather than confirming the selection of a new employee, i.e. induction rather than probation.

Chapter **3**

Getting Started and What Helps

- Starting work in a new organisation
- Orientation
- Establishing a learning continuum
- Key considerations in getting started and what helps in the first few weeks in your new post

The first year in practice, as a qualified professional, is most commonly seen as a period of frenetic activity, in which there is a plethora of information and detail to take on board. Students emerging from different professional training courses – social work, teaching, nursing – readily recognise that there is so much more to know than can be learned in a formal taught course.

66 Nothing can prepare you for this job – ever. (NQSW) **99**

Starting out in a new job is a daunting prospect for anyone, but it can be particularly so if you are taking up your first post in a new profession.

Starting work in a new organisation

Box 3.1 suggests a number of points to help you reflect on your previous experiences of being a new worker. Some new graduates will be joining a completely new employer, whereas others will have undertaken qualification training through a secondment arrangement with their employers, having previously worked for the organisation in an unqualified capacity. It might be thought that seconded workers would be in a better position to hit the ground running, but in our experience we have found that qualified professional status weighs no less heavily on the shoulders of these newly qualified social workers than on those who are facing their first day in a completely new organisation. In fact, if you are starting work following a secondment, it is almost more important that you are able to establish yourself effectively in your new professional role.

Box 3.1 Starting as a new worker

Think of a situation in which you were a new worker – perhaps the first day in the final placement of your qualifying training:

- How were you greeted and by whom?
- What equipment was ready for you on arrival?
- What was particularly welcoming?
- What was missing that would have improved your experience?

Welcome arrangements

On your first day, other than in exceptional circumstances, you should expect to be welcomed by your line manager and to meet your supervisor, if this is going to be someone different. They should be responsible for introducing you to everyone in your team, including senior managers and administrative and clerical staff, as well as social care and social work colleagues. More recently, some organisations have adopted the practice of identifying a particular person in the team who is willing to act as a 'buddy' or mentor to a new member of staff and it can be very helpful in the first few weeks to have someone to whom you may turn for help, information and advice in addition to your formal line manager or supervisor. This is a particularly effective arrangement because those doing the supporting are able to share the load, and you may feel more comfortable because you are not having to go to the same person too often, giving you choice if you find that one person is not available, for whatever reason.

Whatever your route to qualified status has been, obviously you will want to make a good start, and you will be acutely aware of just how important first impressions will be in establishing yourself as a capable and effective member of the team. As far as the organisation is concerned, preparations should begin well before you start work as a new employee. Criteria by which you might judge a good introduction could include some or all of the following.

'Best Practice' guidelines

- Preparation for your arrival which ensures you are expected by the whole team, including reception, clerical and administrative staff.

- The presence of a manager on the first day to make personal introductions.

- Preparation of the team including identifying another team member to act as a named buddy or mentor, to facilitate settling in.

- Preparation of a programme of wider orientation, both within and beyond the immediate team or organisation, including visits and introductions to other team managers, team members and resources.

What will be available to you in terms of equipment, when you start your new job? It would be reasonable to be provided with a few tools of the trade on arrival, and you would normally expect to have the following:

- access to a desk – but bear in mind that in many offices a shared workstation or hot desk is increasingly becoming the norm

- a telephone – make a note of the number and any extension

- a mobile telephone – make a note of the number and clarify the conditions including private or personal use

- a desktop PC or laptop – check security arrangements and passwords

- a diary for appointments

- arrangements for parking your car.

Once you have your letter of appointment, a quick call to your new team manager might be a good idea. In an ideal world, if you are going to be completely new to the organisation, it would be advantageous to arrange a visit to the team in advance of your start date, to give you the chance to get yourself orientated in the building and to ask a few questions to sort out a number of small queries about how everything works and what will happen on the first day. You could use this opportunity to ask about where you will be sitting and the equipment that will be available to you – so that even if the answer is 'not much', or 'don't know yet', at least you will not be harbouring false expectations, and any initial disappointment will have been avoided. Some of your queries might be about very basic information, but often it is not knowing what is expected that can make you feel insecure.

Box 3.2 Day one checklist

The following list suggests some of the things you might like to know about how your new office functions:

- What happens on the first day? Where should I report and at what time?

- Do I need a pass card or security number to get in and out of the building or into the car park?

- What time is the office usually open? If I need access to anything outside of normal working hours, can I get in?

- Where is the staff cloakroom and is there a secure place for my personal belongings?

- Is there a noticeboard or pigeonholes for messages and communications or is everything handled electronically?

- Is there a dress code?

- What are the arrangements for tea and coffee?

You will of course have your own list of questions to which you need answers, and even if you are not going to make a preappointment visit, you should collect your thoughts together by creating your own checklist.

Orientation

For all new staff, a period of initial orientation will be absolutely essential to introduce you to your new surroundings. Good orientation may cover a number of elements, but we would suggest three areas for early attention: the people, the patch and the paperwork.

The people

Take time in the first few days to get to know the names, contact details, job titles and particular areas of responsibility or 'expertise' of each of your new colleagues. You should also try to include members of other teams, units or projects – noting names and contact details – with whom you will be liaising. Some of these will be social workers, but others will be from different professions, particularly health and education, and it will be a good investment to use some of the first few weeks in post in getting to know the important players, and beginning to build your own network of local facilities and resources, both inside and outside your own organisation. Your manager may well suggest it, but you would be well advised in any case to make individual appointments to introduce yourself and to find out, first hand, how best to integrate into existing local networks and make the most useful links with your own role, so that when you are in the midst of a new piece of work and need to make use of a particular service, you already have a good idea of what is available locally and, more importantly, you will already have a named contact.

The patch

This is about getting out and about to familiarise yourself with the geography, demography and general infrastructure of the area in which you will be working. If you are working somewhere which is entirely new to you, you will need to familiarise yourself with a wide range of local facilities, including buses and trains, schools and colleges, job centres, family centres and surgeries, refuges, and youth and community centres, as well as whatever cultural, sport and leisure facilities exist within the locality. This is not an exhaustive list, but is intended as a trigger for the development of your own checklist. There is sometimes no substitute for pounding the pavements to develop a deeper understanding of the neighbourhood and wider environment which forms the context for the lives of residents in your locality, and to imprint some of the important features of 'the patch' in your mind.

The paperwork

It is worth noting here that recent research (Stalker *et al.* 2007) has shown that although service users certainly provoke anxieties in all sorts of ways for newly qualified social workers, this does not translate into quite the same feelings of stress, frustration and sometimes even anger that is experienced as a result of the competing pressures and demands of the procedural arrangements in their organisations, as evidenced by quotations from newly qualified social workers who we talked to.

> **"** You spend all your time thinking about how you're going to get through this [IT] system and how to record it and make a square peg fit into a round hole. (NQSW)
>
> I didn't want to be a typist ... I didn't train to do that. (NQSW)
>
> It's not that I haven't done the work, the work has been done, I just haven't got the time to write it all up every bloody day. (NQSW) **"**

All organisations will have their own information technology (IT) systems, documentation and forms, together with particular procedures for processing, approving and storing them. Unless you have undertaken qualification by secondment or secured employment in the same organisation in which you have had a substantial practice placement as part of your qualifying course, all of this will be new to you and will certainly take time for you to operate confidently within.

Establishing a learning continuum

You might feel that your first year in practice is one in which your performance is endlessly monitored and assessed. With your supervisor or line manager, you should try to shift this emphasis to providing guidance, advice and support for your learning and development. We consider here two mechanisms that you could adopt immediately to contribute to the establishment of a learning continuum.

Using personal development plan (PDP)

In order to lay claim to the title of social worker and enter the professional register, you will have completed an approved programme of academic study leading to the award of the social work degree. The requirements for social work training (Department of Health 2002) make clear that practice must lie at the heart of the new qualifying degree in social work, with academic learning supporting practice rather than the other way around. The *National Occupational Standards for Social Work* (TOPSS UK Partnership 2002) set out what employers require newly qualified social workers to be able to do on entering employment. The 6 key roles, incorporating 21 standards statements, will be very familiar to you as the criteria against which you will have been assessed in your qualifying training programme and Key Role 6 – *Demonstrate professional competence in social work practice* – includes in its standards a requirement to 'ensure own professional development'. Training programmes have generally assisted students to address this requirement by providing graduates with what we are calling a 'personal development plan'. The document itself may have a range of titles and descriptions, specific to each particular training programme, but somewhere towards the end of your final year in training you should have been provided with a summative statement, alongside your transcript of academic achievement, in which areas of particular strength and those requiring further development are identified. Your achievement in relation to each of the national occupational standards will normally have been discussed and written up as part of your final practice portfolio. Because, by definition, the national occupational standards set out the general expectations which employers have of newly qualified social workers, it is your own individual record of achievement against each of the standards that provides you with an immediate link between what you already know and can do, and what will be expected of you in your first employment.

To integrate your qualification more closely into your first employment as a newly qualified social worker, you should ensure that you take the opportunity to provide your supervisor with a copy of your PDP, which can then be used to underpin your initial induction and development within the agency. Ideally, line managers and staff development or training personnel responsible for your 'welcome' to the agency should ask to see your personal development plan, but even if it is not asked for, you could ensure that you produce it and that you are ready to discuss its contents within your supervision sessions. In summary, then, your PDP can be used to:

- transfer baseline information about your present strengths and areas for improvement into the workplace

- provide a helpful starting point for initial supervision discussions with your line manager

- underpin your initial induction and development programme in the agency.

By actively using the personal development plan generated from your qualifying training programme in this way, you have begun the process of personal and professional development which is a fundamental part of your commitment to improving your knowledge and skills. Continuing your professional development will be an ongoing, career-long process, a subject to which we return in more detail in Chapter 12.

Keeping and using a reflexive journal

Your continuing professional development should also be closely related to your own reflections in and on practice – how you feel you are developing at the present time, as well as the directions in which you want to develop in the future. An ideal place to capture your thoughts and ideas is in a reflexive journal. You may already have used a journal, diary or learning log in your qualifying training, and you should not lose the habit just because you are no longer a student. The idea of a reflexive journal is to enable you to have a place in which to collect some of your thoughts and responses to situations or incidents that you encounter in your everyday practice.

You might like to start the journal as soon as you take up your new post. You could begin with:

- an outline of your current role and responsibilities

- a 'skills and needs' analysis in relation to your professional and personal learning – for example, skills you feel you have or wish to develop, and your professional development or other learning needs

- a self-assessment in relation to your knowledge and use of theory and research in practice.

As you progress through your first year, you will be able to revisit your earlier entries in order to evaluate any changes you feel have taken place. The aim of the journal itself is to allow you to reflect on issues related to service users, colleagues or other professionals, and your employing organisation, *as they occur*. However, the primary focus should be on *you*, your thoughts and reactions, rather than on details of the situations themselves.

You could make use of a journal like this in a number of ways:

- to inform the agenda for supervision (your reflections should provide you with some strong material to enable you to focus discussions with your line manager directly on your practice – its difficulties as well as its delights)

- to be a repository of evidence for future use in a post-qualifying portfolio

- to contribute to evidence to meet re-registration requirements

- to contribute to evidence of development as part of performance management and appraisal processes.

You might find the headings in Box 3.3 useful in designing a layout for your journal.

Box 3.3 A reflexive journal or learning log: format suggestion

Key interactions

- What happened?
- Who was involved?
- Where did it take place?
- What was the scale of the incident?

Reflection

- What issues did it raise?
- How did you use theories/knowledge/research/skills?
- What feelings were engendered and how did you manage?
- What tensions, conflicts and stresses emerged and how did you try to address them?
- What issues of difference, discrimination or inequality emerged and how did you work with them?

Future action

- What action might or will you take?
- What might you add to your action plan?
- What might you do differently?

Key considerations in getting started and what helps in the first few weeks in your new post

- Try not to expect too much of yourself – mistakes are an essential part of any learning process and everyone makes them.

- Frame agency processes and procedures, particularly those that are new to you, in a positive way. Approach the paperwork as a framework which can help you to structure your work so that it works for you – not the other way around.

- If you have navigated your way through a degree programme, you have all the computer literacy skills you need to deal effectively and efficiently with your employer's IT system.

- Try to accept that reports do not all have to be perfect – good enough and on time is often a more realistic combination.

- Remember that you are not on your own and that if you are in doubt, ask for advice.

Part II

Warming Up

In Part II, we move on from early orientation to consider some of the priority issues which will present themselves during the next few months. Our focus now is on the more formal corporate and role-specific induction processes in your agency with more about managing your time and planning your personal development.

A key task at this stage, explored in Chapter 4 'Induction', will be formulating a written supervision agreement with your line manager, setting out your respective roles and responsibilities so that you establish a strong, trusting and supportive relationship. We return to wider aspects of supervision and support in Part III.

Learning and development are key themes integrated throughout Part II on 'warming up', as you move away from the information-gathering activities associated with orientation in Part I and embark on your more formal and extended induction programme. Your personal development plan (PDP) from qualification is the key tool for helping you to make the links between your previous experiences, your current work and your future aspirations. We suggest drawing on the national occupational standards to gauge for yourself your growing confidence – separate from competence – and a model for undertaking a self-assessment of your learning needs. Based on the standards for your new post, a self-assessment will help you to identify strengths and turn any gaps into a range of learning objectives with which to update your PDP. You can then use the updated PDP to inform your decisions about the training courses and events which you plan to attend over the coming three to six months, as well as helping you to take the lead in supervision discussions with your line manager about the types of work that you will need to build into your caseload.

Chapter 5 'Roles and Tasks' moves on again to help you manage your initial expectations about roles and tasks and some of the agency demands and bureaucratic burden by focusing your attention on a 'hierarchy of need' with good induction at the bottom of the triangle as the foundation on which you will be able to build your future development.

Managing your tasks and time are the focus in Chapter 6 'Time Management and the Work/Life Balance' as your workload steadily increases, in size and complexity, over the next few months. The importance of managing the boundaries between work and home are emphasised here if you are to establish an appropriate work/life balance for your long-term health and well-being.

Chapter 4

Induction

- Workplace culture
- Corporate induction
- Role-related induction
- Personal development planning
- Key considerations for a successful induction

The section on orientation in Chapter 3 deliberately separated out some of the very early, short-term information-gathering activities vital in the first few weeks to build your knowledge of local networks and resources. Induction processes are concerned with the way in which you are introduced to the more formal requirements of the agency, both as a corporate employee and in relation to the more specific duties and responsibilities of your particular role within the organisation. Induction in this sense will not be complete in the first few weeks in practice – it is more likely to be a programme of activities that will carry on throughout your first year in post.

The majority of NQSWs experience their first year in practice as a tough and testing time, underlining the need for good support during this crucial transition period.

Workplace culture

In the present context of public services across the UK, in which funding is often closely tied to successfully meeting performance targets set by central government, the workplace culture of many organisations employing social workers routinely prioritises operational efficiency and accountability over the well-being and professional development of their staff. In effect this frequently means that the *quantity* of their activities and outputs is deemed to be more important than the *quality* of the work that they do. Of course, even in the present policy context there are exceptions to this general rule, exemplified by employers that recognise the value of nurturing and developing their staff, within the overall culture of what is often referred to as a 'learning organisation'. It is in these organisations that you are likely to find the best arrangements for your induction as a newly qualified social worker. There is more on learning organisations in Chapter 11.

You can go some way towards assessing the strength of the learning culture in your own workplace by answering the questions relating to the arrangements for your induction in Box 4.1.

Box 4.1 Understanding the learning culture of your workplace

- Does the agency have a written induction policy? Do I have a copy?

- Does my job description include professional development, PQ and PRTL?

- Is time allocated with my line manager for discussion of induction and development issues?

- Am I clear about which parts of the organisation (operational manager, staff development or training department) can help in identifying my learning needs and opportunities to meet them?

- Am I encouraged to use my personal development plan (PDP) effectively in relation to the requirements of my new post?

If the answer to any of these questions is 'No', it would be sensible to discuss the issue with your supervisor or line manager.

Where you assess your employer's commitment to professional development is relatively weak, there are some positive early steps that you can take to establish your own 'learning culture', including the following:

- discussing your PDP in supervision

- seeking opportunities to try out knowledge and skills acquired from training in the new pieces of work allocated to you (in discussion with your line manager)

- linking the in-house training you attend to the areas for development identified in your PDP

- maintaining a reflexive journal from which you can extract issues for discussion in supervision, and use as a source of evidence in NQSW or post-qualifying programmes, or as a contribution to your PRTL record.

Corporate induction

Corporate induction programmes, particularly in large organisations such as local authorities, are commonly coordinated and delivered by the staff development or training unit, and will be set up according to a pre-scheduled timetable. Depending on when you start, there may be a programme for you to attend within the first few weeks, and this is certainly a good time to get a broader picture of the organisation as a whole, and of where you sit within its structures. Corporate induction will generally deal with issues that are common to all staff who are new to the organisation, and the topics normally covered are included in the checklist in Box 4.2.

As the short checklist reveals, much of the content of this type of corporate induction is limited to information-giving, and while it can be helpful to have this level of detail as early as possible, it might be quite a relief not to be asked to take on more information in the first few weeks at work, when you may already be feeling the effects of 'information overload'. There is a growing reliance on placing policies and procedures on web-based intranets, and this does mean in principle that documents are readily available for you to view at a time that is convenient for you. However, computer facilities are not always available to new staff in the first few weeks in post. Even when you have access to the system, you may still have to deal with the frustration of trying to locate a document that appears to be hidden deep within the organisation's intranet. It is a good idea, then, to use the corporate induction sessions to try to collect as many policies and procedure documents in paper format as you can and to ensure that you are clear exactly where and how the various policies and procedures referred to in any sessions you attend can be accessed afterwards.

Box 4.2 Corporate induction: checklist

Although not exhaustive, the following list brings together the key elements that you should expect to find as part of any corporate induction programme.

- Organisational structure
- Mission statement – goals, values and priorities of the organisation
- Personnel policies: health and safety; annual leave; sickness; data protection
- Finance policies and procedures: pay; pension; travel; expenses
- Codes of conduct, grievance and disciplinary procedures
- Performance management and appraisal processes

Role-related induction

A properly structured programme of induction, agreed in consultation with your manager, should include the following:

- recognising areas of existing experience, knowledge and strength (which makes links with your personal development plan)

- drawing up a comprehensive list of people and places to visit (as already considered in Chapter 3)

- identifying documentation and literature to read (including handbooks and operating manuals, and examples of written work, such as case notes, assessment forms and court reports, to familiarise yourself with the style and standards that apply within the agency)

- developing a structure and timetable for the programme (that integrates corporate elements of induction with more role-specific requirements).

As the following quotes illustrate, many agencies invest significant resources in their induction packages, including the provision of a range of training courses. Unfortunately, as the second quote suggests, not all ensure that their induction programmes for NQSWs are part of a coherent overall workforce strategy, in which close links are made between the delivery of high quality services and the role-related and continuing professional development needs of their staff, with the result that much of the value of any initial investment may be lost.

> " I've worked for private companies and I cannot think of one company I've worked for who've invested the same kind of money that this local authority has invested in me ... They've invested a huge amount. (NQSW)
>
> The agency are committed to it, yes, they can do the financial bit, but in terms of all the other things, it's not there. (NQSW) "

Successful induction requires an active partnership between operational managers and staff development personnel, as part of strategies to promote an overall 'learning organisation', in which there is good communication across all levels of the organisation.

In parallel with the corporate processes, role-specific induction for NQSWs should address the issues which are more closely related to your particular job and the expectations, duties and responsibilities of your qualified social worker role. It ought to be:

- coordinated with what is available at a more corporate level

- standardised across the agency, to cover activities during your first 12 months in post

- linked to your personal development plan, including learning opportunities and continuing professional development arrangements.

A structured induction programme

The checklist in Box 4.3, and the sections which follow it, provide a guide to the content of a well-planned, role-related induction programme.

Box 4.3 Role-related induction: checklist

You should expect your induction programme (discussed and agreed with your manager) to include the following:

- A named person responsible for your induction programme
- A reduced and protected caseload
- Good quality supervision that is regular and planned
- Consideration of re-registration requirements and codes of practice
- An organisational structure diagram
- Agency procedures manual(s)
- Personal development planning

A named person responsible for your agency induction programme

Although in some cases this task may be delegated to a member of the staff development or training unit, which can be useful for making these wider connections in the early stages of your appointment, there really needs to be close involvement with your line manager and/or supervisor. It is vital that your line manager is aware of the content, pace and timetable of your induction programme so that, as well as monitoring and reviewing your progress, your workload can be tailored to your needs and built up around the development opportunities you have been offered. It is well recognised that learning is most effectively consolidated when you have a chance to try out in practice, as soon as possible after returning to your workplace, something new that you have learned as part of a training course, and your line manager will be best placed to provide this central link between induction activities and your developing workload. You can assist by ensuring that these links are reviewed and progressed in supervision.

A reduced and protected workload

This should mean that responsibilities and allocated cases or other tasks are built up gradually, taking account of your previous experience and strengths, as well as the programme of learning and development agreed as part of your specific induction. There are strong links to be made here with your personal development plan from qualification.

The best induction programmes will offer a case-free introductory period, in which you will be able to undertake orientation and information-gathering tasks, as well as spending time with your new team, just observing how things work on a day-to-day basis and absorbing something of the workplace culture. This introductory period might also provide opportunities for shadowing or co-working with more experienced social workers or other professionals, to increase your awareness of relevant legislation, protocols, procedures and processes in particular situations, and opportunities to observe the communication and engagement skills being used by more experienced colleagues. An introductory period like this might also give you the opportunity to read through case notes, recordings, assessments and reports that others have produced, to help familiarise you with the structure, content and quality that is expected in written work for your agency.

Even if you do not have the luxury of a completely case-free introduction, it would be unusual now, as a newly qualified worker, not to have some reduction in the size of your workload for an initial period. In all probability, a reduced caseload will be defined using a range of criteria related to the team and setting in which you are working. Calculations may be simply numerical – the number of children, young people and families – or may take account of other factors, such as process stage, risk and complexity. Whatever caseload management system is used, you should ensure that you understand how your caseload has been structured, and that you are clear about how any policy on reduction is going to be implemented and brought to an end. Ideally, this should be a flexible process, reviewed and updated regularly in supervision discussions with your line manager, in the light of your own progress and how the work allocated to you is developing. Guidance relevant to this area has been offered in England by the Children's Workforce Development Council's NQSW Pilot Programme (CWDC 2008b), which specifies that newly qualified staff should not be expected to take on the same level of responsibility as other social workers, and in their first year in post should carry 90 per cent of the work 'that a confident second or third year social worker would undertake'. Arrangements for co-working and shadowing are included in the 90 per cent expectation.

As well as some reduction in the *size* of your caseload in the early stages of your employment, protection from some *types of work* should also be arranged. It would be reasonable to expect that the level of work allocated to you in the first few weeks would be similar to the sort of work that you undertook as a final year student. Protection will be particularly relevant in areas of work to which you were not exposed as a student, for example child protection and court work. Again, you need to ensure that you are clear about the policies that exist, and the ways in which they will be applied to you. Shadowing and co-working in these protected areas, with guidance and advice from more experienced staff, are good ways in which you can build up your knowledge and confidence in new areas of work.

The CWDC pilot programmes in England also specify that 10 per cent of a NQSW's time must be ring-fenced for professional development activities. For those working full-time, this equates to a half-day each week in which you should have freedom to pursue some aspect of your development plan – for instance attending courses, reading, researching, or attending peer mentoring or support groups. See Box 4.4.

Box 4.4 A reduced and protected workload: checklist

Key areas for agreement with your manager:

- Case-free introduction

- Reduced caseload (e.g. 90 per cent of normal caseload)

- Protected caseload (complexity and risk building on your stage of development and previous experiences)

- Protection of time (half-day per week for professional development)

- Shadowing (to build knowledge and understanding in protected areas of practice)

- Co-working (to build confidence in more complex areas, without case responsibility)

- Changes to caseload linked to development plan (PDP) discussed in supervision

---

Supervision

There is little doubt that supervision is of paramount importance to all professionally qualified social workers, and Chapter 9 is dedicated entirely to this subject, but it is hardly possible to consider induction without giving some attention to the initial arrangements for your supervision. Good quality, planned supervision, which takes place on a regular basis, is an important learning and support mechanism at all stages of professional development. As a student, you will already have experienced a variety of styles and approaches to supervision, but at that time you will also have had the support and guidance of a practice teacher, as well as course tutors and the student group of which you were a member.

To be effective, supervision needs to include consideration of *your* needs, not solely those of your employing organisation. All social workers, regardless of their experience, will have particular needs at different times, and you should avoid any tendency to regard supervision as a process only for dealing with problems. Access to supervision is your right as a professional worker, in accordance with official codes of practice (e.g. General Social Care Council (GSCC) 2002, Code 2.2), and you must be ready to take full advantage of the opportunities available to you. It will also be written into your contract of employment, and you should ensure that you are clear about its functions. Supervision is a process which should enable you to learn and grow, both personally and professionally, as well as supporting you in dealing with the stresses and pressures of the job. If your agency has a policy that defines supervision and clarifies expectations, it is important that you familiarise yourself with it.

Several definitions of supervision exist, each identifying a range of aims and objectives, but with brevity in mind, Table 4.1 provides a useful summary of the three most widely accepted aspects.

Table 4.1 Supervision: summary of aims and functions

Aim	Function
To enable you to carry out your work effectively	Organisational/managerial
To develop your practice through lifelong learning and professional development	Professional/educational
To support and help you address the emotional pressures and stress of the work	Personal/interpersonal

During your induction period you should expect to have more frequent supervision than will be available to you as an established professional. In England the CWDC (2008b) suggests that supervision for an NQSW should take place every two weeks during the first three months in post, reducing to monthly after that. It is also suggested that each session should be about an hour and a half long.

Supervision should be tailored to each person's stage of development, confidence and abilities, the learning opportunities undertaken, and the range of work and level of responsibility held. The supervisor–supervisee relationship is an important one, and how you are going to work together will need to be established in a clear and unambiguous way. As pointed out by Morrison (2001), a written contract will have been the basis for your practice learning as a student, and there is no reason why your supervision as an NQSW should not take place within a similarly structured, written agreement. In the early stages of your professional development, clear structures, practical information and emotional support are all important elements that will provide you with reassurance about your practice, and a supervisor who has a positive, tolerant and approachable style will be best placed to offer you effective help. As a new worker you are likely to have a limited range of practice experience on which to draw, so that each piece of work may take you into unfamiliar territory, presenting new and sometimes perplexing challenges. As we saw in Chapter 1, these new experiences begin to become more manageable as you move from practice guided by context-free rules, to the development of your own set of situational rules. The ability to see wider patterns in the work that you are undertaking will be developing, but in these early days you are likely to be dealing with each piece of work somewhat separately, focusing closely on the details of each new situation. Supervision can provide the time and support you need to be able to make the links between different cases and experiences, facilitating the process of ordering and prioritising particular elements.

As an NQSW at the start of your career, no doubt with high expectations of yourself, it is easy to become over-sensitised to any minor failings that may occur. In these circumstances, it is not unusual to find yourself overwhelmed by emotion at times, and supervision should help you to reflect on your expectations of yourself, ensuring that they are realistic. Remember to focus as much on what went right and was successful, as on what may have gone wrong. Try to use supervision to help you to reframe any feelings of 'failure' as a natural part of your professional development. Learning from challenging situations will often remain indelibly etched in your memory, and it is from these experiences, given appropriate time for reflection and recovery through supervision, that the greatest practice improvements often occur.

There are many examples of written contracts for supervision, and if your agency has an overarching supervision policy, this may include a preferred format. However, if you find that your employing agency does not provide any guidance, you might find the checklist in Box 4.5 helpful.

Box 4.5 Supervision agreement: checklist

You may find the following suggestions helpful as headings for discussion with your line manager to develop a written agreement for supervision:

- Agenda setting – responsibilities and arrangements
- Frequency, duration and venue
- Permitted interruptions
- Method of recording
- Confidentiality – what is to remain confidential; what can be discussed elsewhere
- Expectations and contribution of supervisor and supervisee
- Use of personal development plan
- Arrangements for dealing with problems within supervision
- Date for review of the agreement
- Signatures of both parties

More important than the document's format is that the agreement should be arrived at through negotiation, so that issues that are likely to arise and how they will be addressed and managed within the process are clearly identified.

Professional registration and codes of practice

Re-registration requirements are clearly linked to your personal development plan and to the ongoing improvement of professional standards. Registration brought with it the 'thud' that we considered in Chapter 1, and the requirements for periodic re-registration could well arrive with a similar shock if you do not keep a written record of your learning and development. Establishing good habits from the very beginning will pay dividends a bit further down the line. You should try to familiarise yourself with exactly what is required by the Care Council relevant to the country in which you are working (a brief outline of the requirements for re-registration with each of the councils in the four UK countries is included in Chapter 12, Table 12.1, and specific guidelines are available on their respective websites). Post-registration training and learning (PRTL), which is an essential part of re-registration, is the place where you are required to formally confirm your commitment to learning throughout your professional career. Larger employers are likely to have recording systems, probably on their intranet, that will help you maintain an appropriate portfolio of evidence, and it would be a good idea to check out before you start what help might be available to you, but in the final analysis, it is the individual responsibility of each professional social worker to maintain a PRTL record. A simple ring binder is all that is needed to begin with, in which you can store in one place a record of texts and journals you have read; website and other online materials you have consulted; courses, conferences and seminars you have attended; and presentations you have made to the team, other colleagues or service users and carers. Later on, some of the information which you have already collected for PRTL purposes will also feed directly into your personal development plan, as well as into the agency's appraisal and performance management systems. It is also worth checking if your employers will meet your re-registration fees. There is more about PRTL in Chapter 12.

Over recent years, the regulatory bodies in the four countries that make up the UK have each developed codes of practice for social workers and their employers. Among other things, these codes require that social workers are personally accountable for the quality of their work. This means that you are under an obligation to tell your employer (and seek appropriate help) if you consider that you are not competent to perform any of the tasks that have been allocated to you. The regulatory bodies also publish reports about the nature of any complaints made against social workers under their respective codes. At the time of writing, the most recent report published by the General Social Care

Council for England (2008a) revealed that the most frequent cause of complaint from those who use services or members of the public was in relation to poor professional practice, such as the social worker 'lied in their report' or 'was biased' or 'failed to ensure that I got my care package' (GSCC 2008a, p.15). However, the second most frequent cause of complaint arose from allegations of inappropriate relationships between social workers and people who use services. As an NQSW, it is therefore important that you maintain appropriate, professional relationships at all times with people who use services. Concerns would arise if there are certain individuals or groups of service users for whom you take on extra things, and some for whom you do not. Are you setting up unfair expectations that other staff might have to cope with? Are you treating people with respect, dignity and fairness? What are your motives? A good indicator to guide your behaviour is never to do anything that you feel you could not tell your manager. If you cannot tell others what you are doing, then you probably should not be doing it.

Organisational structure diagram

This should help to clarify relevant line management and reporting responsibilities, both horizontally and vertically, through the various tiers of the organisation. It is important that you are able to clearly identify your place and that of your team and your manager in relation to the wider organisation. As you become more established in the workplace, knowledge of organisational structures and processes is likely to have an increasingly important influence on your practice. Using such knowledge to promote best practice is an integral part of what might be termed the 'political' aspect of organisational life, and those who understand how organisations work will be well placed to achieve outcomes and promote changes for the benefit of service users and carers, as well as themselves and their colleagues.

Procedures manuals

Procedures manuals should help you to build your knowledge and understanding of the way in which the organisation functions in key areas. Those detailing professional procedures should provide information about the framework for practice agreed within your employing agency. A well-produced manual will give you clear guidance about relevant areas of your work, providing information about the application of legislation and policy, assessment frameworks and thresholds, information-sharing protocols, decision-making processes, and safe working practices, particularly in relation to lone working. There may also be separate manuals which provide guidance about the agency's various administrative processes, including the forms needed for each task. Frustration with bureaucracy can be avoided if you know what form is needed for a specific task, and where to look for it. It is advisable to get hold of written copies of any manuals used in your employing agency (in addition to web-based versions) since these are often lengthy documents which are not easy to digest on screen, and you may need to refer to them alongside other documents on your computer.

Personal development planning

Throughout this chapter we have referred to the centrality of learning in your professional development. Rather like the supervision agreement discussed earlier, the personal development plan (PDP) with which you graduated requires periodic review and updating if it is to play an active role in guiding your continuing professional development. The process of personal development planning can be understood as a cyclical process, as illustrated in Figure 4.1.

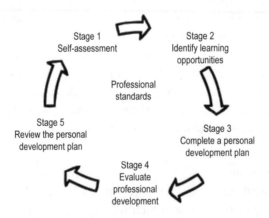

Figure 4.1 Personal development plan process (reproduced from Noakes *et al.* 1998)

Self-assessment

The process suggested here (Noakes *et al.* 1998) begins with a self-assessment against the professional standards relevant to your post (e.g. NQSW programme outcomes, PQ consolidation module learning outcomes). The intention of this stage in the PDP process is to help you to think about how your previous experience and learning matches up with the demands of your new job. To do this, it is helpful to ask yourself three questions against *each* standard being considered:

- What knowledge, skills and values do I already have in this area?
- What do I need to learn to address any gaps?
- How am I going to learn the new things I have identified?

You might find it helpful to record your self-assessment in tabular form, as set out in Table 4.2.

Table 4.2 A self-assessment form for each professional standard

Professional standard		
Stage I: What do I already know?	What direct teaching have I had in relation to this standard?	For example: Qualifying training modules Seminars In-house courses Directed reading
	What other experiences have contributed to my knowledge about this standard?	For example: Work experiences Personal experiences Placements Reading, researching
Stage 2: What do I need to learn?	What gaps do I have in relation to this standard? What needs strengthening?	For example: Use of legislation, policy Multi-agency working Use of frameworks Agency procedures Specific skills
Stage 3: How am I going to learn it?	What work or other learning opportunities would meet the gaps I have identified?	For example: Types of cases Ways of working (observation, co-working, shadowing) Courses or training Resource packs or manuals Supervision Learning sets

Designing your PDP

The gaps identified in Stage 2 above define the areas for development which are carried into Stage 3 of the cycle, and become the objectives to be met in your PDP. When you have identified your objectives, the checklist in Box 4.6 can be used to record the arrangements agreed with your manager or training department for your continuing professional development.

Box 4.6 Designing your PDP: checklist

Use the following questions in relation to each of your learning objectives to record your personal development plan in tabular form:

- What do I want to achieve?
- What sort of activity is involved?
- How soon do I need to do this (start date and expected completion)?
- What resources do I need (e.g. release, backfill, course costs)?
- Who can help me (e.g. Human Resources (HR), colleagues, other agency/ professional)?
- How will I know when I have achieved this objective?
- How and where will evidence be recorded and stored?

Finalising the first draft of your PDP will necessitate some detailed discussions with your line manager or supervisor, to prioritise the learning you need to undertake and to agree how and when the range of activities identified will be made available to you. The aim is to design a coherent pathway which explicitly links your evolving workload with your personal progress and the training opportunities planned for you. If it is going to be a useful tool, your PDP needs to be used on a regular basis, by both you and your manager or supervisor. Stage 4 of the PDP process is concerned with evaluating your progress, and you can therefore use your PDP to monitor your progress in supervision and in the agency's formal appraisal processes. The outcomes from these discussions will then be recorded in a revised PDP (Stage 5) bringing the full personal planning cycle back to Stage 1 again, at which point you undertake a new self-assessment of your learning needs as the next step in your continuing professional development. We link up again with this cyclical process in Chapter 12.

Key considerations for a successful induction

- Take the lead in ensuring that you discuss your PDP from qualification in supervision with your line manager.

- Formulate a written supervision agreement with your line manager, setting out your respective roles and responsibilities.

- Undertake a self-assessment of your learning needs in relation to the standards relevant for your new post, identifying any gaps and suggesting a concrete plan to meet them.

- Use the objectives identified in your (updated) PDP to make links to the training courses you plan to attend and the types of work you are undertaking.

Chapter 5

Roles and Tasks

:' Definition of social work

:' Initial expectations

:' Personal motivations

:' Initial confidence

:' Core tasks

:' Key considerations about roles and tasks

Having looked at induction, we now go on in this chapter to explore some of the intended roles and tasks of social work with children and families, and how these are linked to your motivations to join the social work profession in the first place. We take a look at your initial workplace confidence – as opposed to competence – against the national occupational standards, and turn to your initial expectations, exploring some of the early tensions between these and the demands of your organisation.

Definition of social work

On the face of it, a definition of social work would be a logical place to start thinking about roles and tasks. However, there is in fact no definition of social work to which all groups within the profession will readily assent. Attempts to define what its proper activities should be, how its membership should be trained, what criteria should be applied to recruitment and so on become perennially entwined with long-standing debates about the centrality of particular theories, methods or principles, disputes about roles or functions, and disagreement about responsibility for an almost unending array of practical tasks – all of which play a part, but none of which is sufficient on its own to describe what is expected of the profession by employers or by qualified social workers themselves, in the wide range of contexts in which they operate.

In England, the General Social Care Council, in association with the Commission for Social Care Inspection, the Children's Workforce Development Council and the Social Care Institute for Excellence and Skills for Care, has published a statement of roles and tasks for the twenty-first century (GSCC 2008b) which makes use of the international definition of social work:

> The social work profession promotes social change, problem solving in human relationships and the empowerment and liberation of people to enhance well-being. Utilising theories of human behaviour and social systems, social work intervenes at the points where people interact with their environments. Principles of human rights and social justice are fundamental to social work. (GSCC 2008b, p.9)

The GSCC statement of roles and tasks goes on to provide a number of lists of possible functions, outcomes, tasks and 'situations in which it is recommended that experienced social workers should always be involved'. These make a helpful contribution to understanding the overall context in which social workers currently operate, and point to the contributions that social work can make to policy debates and development, but are rather too general to provide practical guidance about workplace expectations for those new to the profession.

However, differences in the way that services are provided within the four UK nations mean that a number of differences are also developing in relation to the future role of social work in each country. In England, for example, there is an increasing division between adult and children's services, with ever closer links between child care and education, while Scotland has continued with a single social work department, encompassing children, adults and youth justice, and Northern Ireland has maintained the concept of a generic social worker with a closely integrated working relationship with health. A report to the Scottish Executive (2006) suggests that social workers should not undertake tasks that do not require their level of training and skills, and introduces a new para-professional role.

Similar proposals have been made to the Welsh Assembly, suggesting that professional experience could be used more effectively in a redefined workforce, freeing highly qualified staff to undertake the tasks that only they can do while being supported by people undertaking a narrower range of less demanding functions (Welsh Assembly Government 2007). The Platt Review in England has suggested exploration of a generic community care worker role as well as the possibility of a new 'hybrid' role of children's professional and a child protection 'specialist' (Platt 2007).

Initial expectations

Newly qualified social workers are sometimes shocked by the limited amount of time that they get to undertake direct work with service users. Indeed, a major complaint from frontline social workers employed in all settings, but most particularly in local authorities, is that their work has become more bureaucratic and less client focused in recent years (Community Care 2005; Jones 2001; McLenachan 2006; Statham, Cameron and Mooney 2006). Stalker *et al.* (2007) have identified that, even at times of considerable turbulence, 'work with clients' is the factor which contributes most to job satisfaction, and that the degree to which individual workers feel that they have made a difference in people's lives is an important factor in sustaining their morale. It is not difficult to see the roots of these beliefs and satisfactions in the reasons which social workers give for making their choice of career, and it will be important to review your balance of time use as you build up your workload and the focus of work in each case changes and develops.

A long-standing area of concern and frustration for many social workers is the weight of the paperwork with which they are required to deal. The reviews of social work undertaken in England (GSCC 2008b), Scotland (Scottish Executive 2006) and Wales (Association of Directors for Social Services (ADSS) 2005) all report on the pressures of bureaucracy caused by complex forms, problematic IT systems and performance management processes, and a survey of social workers in England found that 80 per cent of respondents considered that reducing the administrative burden should be a priority for the government's workforce review (Community Care 2005). More than half of the respondents to this survey reported spending at least 60 per cent of their time on administrative work, and the volume of paperwork, among other things, caused 90 per cent of practitioners to work longer than their contracted hours on a regular basis, a practice also common among people we have spoken to.

> " Yes, at the moment, I'm probably only putting in about 4 or 5 hours overtime a week ... the way social workers keep on top of their caseload is by working more than 37 hours a week. If you keep to the 37 hours you're paid for, you don't get done what needs to be done. (NQSW) "

By contrast, the national agreement on raising standards and tackling workload for teachers (Department for Education and Skills (DfES) 2003) was specifically designed to reduce the excessive workload that entailed teachers spending two-thirds of their time on administrative tasks. Given this precedent for a national agreement, focused clearly on very specific workload issues, for a similar professional group working with children and young people, it is all the more lamentable that such aims and outcomes have not been replicated, so far, for social workers. However, it is hoped that the Social Work Taskforce, due to report after the writing of this book, will lead to the introduction of similar reforms in social work.

Managing the bureaucratic burden

So what can be done with the bureaucratic burden for social workers? The roles and tasks review in England does refer to the need for employers to provide good quality IT and management systems (GSCC 2008b, p.9). One of the problems associated with the current IT systems is that they are not flexible enough, for example restricting the amount of information that can be entered.

> " It's getting used to what the paperwork's like because I find it very constricting, having to sort everything into boxes. My boss is always saying 'make the boxes work for you' and that's very true. What I think she means by it is – understand what it's asking for and put in, in your own way. So having other colleagues around to talk to has helped. (NQSW) "

Make sure that you seek out training on your own IT system as soon as possible. Give yourself some time just to experiment with it, to become familiar with its commands and to navigate around it. Also try to get access to the forms, reports and records of a more experienced member of staff to give you a better idea of how others are using the system, but making it work for you is the priority here.

Another common frustration in this area is the incompatibility between systems in different organisations, so that the transfer or sharing of information is not a straightforward process. The roll-out of the Integrated Children's System (DfES 2006), and its wider use across health and education in local authority and the independent, voluntary and private sectors, was intended to make a positive contribution. However, this is another issue on the agenda of the Social Work Taskforce as there have been significant problems with its implementation.

For NQSWs, the IT skills needed to complete a degree should more than meet the standard required for most agency systems. Sometimes, the know how is there in principle, but has to be delivered using unfamiliar processes within the constraints of limited time and resources. As recognised by the NQSW quoted here, part of the socialisation process will be about accepting the tensions that inevitably exist at first.

> **''** I've learnt very quickly that you know what actually happens is a far cry from how we would ideally work with people and the restrictions in respect to resources and funding and what we can put in to support families. So I'm taking a deep breath and go, OK, if this what I've got to work with, what can I do with it? (NQSW) **''**

Consider what use you are able to make of other resources. Are there administrative or clerical staff who can assist with data input? Are you able to delegate responsibility for some record-keeping to others, while still retaining proper oversight and case responsibility?

Personal motivations

Career choice

Clearly, your motivations for choosing social work as a career will have some bearing on your initial expectations and ultimate job satisfaction. Little research exists in this area, with one of the only studies to have explored the motivations of new recruits to social work having been undertaken in the early 1970s (Pearson 1973). Nonetheless, the findings appear to be as valid nowadays as they were in the 1970s, and echo our own experience of hearing the reason most often quoted for choosing social work as a profession was 'wanting to help people – to make a difference', with little or no mention of personal career aspirations, higher status or improved income.

> **❝** I may not be able to effect a lot of change but for me, personally, I want to see that I actually try to make some sort of difference. (NQSW)
>
> It's the only reason I do this job really. I mean the money is part of it. Of course it is. It's a job. But I wouldn't be doing it for the money I get paid if I didn't actually want to try and make a difference to people's lives, because I do. And that's the thing that holds me to the job. (NQSW) **❞**

Pearson (1973) contended that those making the choice of social work as a profession in the early 1970s were rejecting normal aspirations for those joining the professions, like the acquisition of money, position or power, in favour of self-actualisation achieved through working for others. He further postulated that social workers' choice of career was an attempt to find a solution to the problems of society at large – in short, an attempt to 'inject dignity and authenticity into a life which threatens to be short on meanings' (p.217). How far do your own motivations match those of the social workers in the studies discussed here?

Achieving potential: hierarchy of needs

While you will almost certainly be familiar with Maslow's (1943) hierarchy of needs in relation to social work with service users, you may not have considered that the ascending stages towards achieving full potential might be equally relevant to your motivation to take up your career. Figure 5.1 sets this out, with your *basic needs* (met through a good induction) acting as the foundation on which the remainder of your professional development rests. In ascending order, this then involves establishing your *safety*, including arrangements for the supervision of your practice, and a sense of *belonging* to the team, organisation and

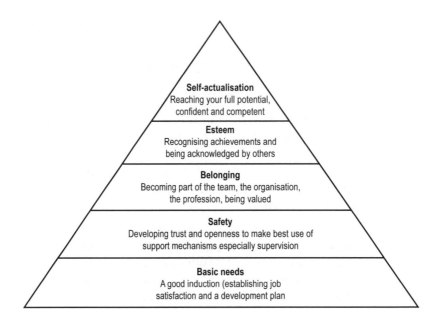

Figure 5.1 Achieving professional potential (adapted from Maslow 1943)

profession of which you are now a member. Once these needs are met, you can then move on to building your personal *esteem*, involving the recognition of your achievements so far, and, finally, the *self-actualisation* posited by Pearson (1973), when you are aspiring to reach your full potential as a confident and competent professional.

Initial confidence

Initial confidence in the workplace cannot be entirely separated from the way in which qualifying training is organised and delivered. The 'specialism versus generic' debate in relation to social work education and training has raged for many decades now (Barclay 1982; Seebohm 1968) and looks set to continue as the fit between the new degree and the requirements of the children's workforce is reviewed. The existing generic degree programmes require social work students to be competent in relation to a comprehensive set of national occupational standards (NOS) (TOPSS UK Partnership 2002), assessed in at least two different practice settings.

However, as we have noted earlier, the 'thud' that comes with the change in status from student to professional should not be underestimated. Socialisation into any new profession is a slow process in which the learning is qualitatively different from being a student, involving the application of skills and knowledge in practice situations where full case responsibility is held. Theories of adult learning (e.g. Schön 1983) help to make the links between learning and experience more explicit. In terms of your own professional development, it is clearly not enough to defer to the opinions of others; you must establish your own know how, which will mean reflecting critically upon your own developing experience, wrestling with the apparent anarchy of the workplace, and increasingly experimenting with your own ideas. Observation and discussion are useful developmental tools, but over time – and with support – your ultimate goal will be gaining the confidence to judge matters from your own perspective, finding what works best for you.

Professional competence

In accepting your name onto their respective registers, the social care councils in the four countries that make up the UK are confirming that you are 'fully competent' to perform the role of social worker. However, we have already noted that whatever is learned in qualifying training represents only the beginning of professional learning, as noted by a newly qualified social worker.

" I begin to realise that there is so much more that I don't know than I do. (NQSW) "

A number of studies of professional development in health and social care (e.g. Eraut 1994; Yelloly and Henkel 1995) have suggested that the development of professional competence takes place on both a conscious and unconscious level. If competence can be both conscious and unconscious, then it follows that incompetence can also develop in these two domains, as represented in Figure 5.2.

Conscious competence	Conscious incompetence
• What I know I know • What I know I can do • Clear transferable skills • Can be easily explained to others	• Openly acknowledged gaps
Unconscious competence	Unconscious incompetence
• What I know or can do without being conscious of how I know it • Hard to explain to others • May be lost in times of turbulence or disruption and change	• Things which I am unaware I do not know • Others may see gaps but I do not

Figure 5.2 A competence matrix (Morrison 2001)

The real danger area identified in the matrix is that of 'unconscious incompetence' as it is here that dangerous practice can take root. It is almost self-evident that, if professional learning develops by doing the job, then the quality and culture of your workplace will have a powerful influence over the ways in which your professional competence is shaped. The greater your exposure to critically reflective evidence-based practice, clearly articulated values, and cooperative working relationships, the more likely you will be to establish good habits, working styles and beliefs. By contrast, the habits developed in a stressed or dysfunctional working environment will tend to foster some elements of unconscious incompetence.

National occupational standards

When you enter your new workplace, you may find it helpful to undertake an assessment of your initial confidence (as distinct from competence) against each of the areas of practice identified in the national occupational standards for social work in the country in which you are working, using a scale like that provided in Box 5.1 (for England).

In our own experience, NQSWs indicate that they feel most confident in areas that were generally linked to skills in helping, advocacy, networking and promoting development and change, and it is not difficult to see how these areas resonate with the personal attitudes,

Box 5.1 Assessing your confidence against national occupational standards

Using the scale of 1 (low) to 10 (high), rate your confidence against each area of practice:

- Which three areas are particular strengths?
- Which three areas are priorities for further development?

If you can, ask your buddy/mentor/supervisor to do the same.

- Do the areas you have identified match those highlighted by your buddy/mentor/ supervisor?
- Can you use the areas for development in identifying learning opportunities? In your PDP? In informal discussions with a buddy or mentor? More formally, in supervision?

	Preparing, producing, implementing and evaluating plans	Assessing needs to recommend a course of action	Responding to crisis situations	Working with individuals and communities – to help them make informed decisions	Working with individuals and communities – to achieve change	Working with groups – to promote development and independence	Supporting networks – to meet assessed needs	Advocating on behalf of individuals and communities	Assessing and managing risks – to individuals and communities	Assessing and managing risks – to self and colleagues	Researching, analysing and using current knowledge of best practice	Preparing for and participating in decision-making forums	Liaising with other teams, professionals, networks and systems	Managing and being accountable for your own work	Managing complex ethical issues, dilemmas and conflicts	Contributing to the management of resources and services
10																
9																
8																
7																
6																
5																
4																
3																
2																
1																

values and motivations for entering social work already discussed, in which you are likely to have had some pre-qualifying experiences.

However, when managers are asked the same question, their views, perhaps unsurprisingly, reflect a greater emphasis on the agency's statutory requirements and the day-to-day pressures of the work. For example, line managers feel that newly qualified social workers are least confident in assessing needs to recommend a course of action, assessing and managing risks to individuals and communities, managing complex ethical issues, and responding to crises. When considered more closely, these areas are also those to which newly qualified social workers may have had more limited exposure as students. It would follow in these circumstances that time will be needed to build a range of practice experiences on which situational rules, as the basis for sound judgement and decision-making, can be founded.

Core tasks

Social workers often refer to the variety of their work as a positive motivator, and the 14 core tasks identified in Box 5.2 attest to the wide range of activities which might commonly be encompassed in a single day in the life of a social worker.

In any job there are, on the one hand, the parts that we enjoy quite naturally, and with which we can engage with real enthusiasm. On the other hand, there will always be elements which we find more challenging or less interesting, which will require more explicit effort and determination. Especially when you are under pressure, it can be these irritating or worrisome elements only that remain etched in your mind. This is rather succinctly expressed by an anonymous aphorist who wrote that 'happiness writes white' (i.e. it is invisible), leaving you with the impression that everything at work is characterised by some degree of difficulty. To avoid developing a distorted impression of your day-to-day activities, it can therefore be helpful to gather some hard data of how you actually spend your own time at work, by filling in Box 5.2 over a period of two weeks. You can use this information not only to reflect on your own initial expectations about, for example, the amount of time you actually do spend doing direct work with service users, but also to inform supervision discussions about your overall workload, type of work, and future development opportunities.

Box 5.2 Time spent on core tasks

What tasks take up your time?

Keeping a record of core tasks over a period of, say, two weeks will help you to see more broadly how you are spending your time.

		Working with parents/carers	Working with children	Working with groups and communities	Preparing reports for boards, panels, court	Evaluating and analysing assessment	Data entry; information management systems	Admin: correspondence/email	Liaising with other professionals	Liaising within team or agency	Supervision	Training/CPD activities	Allocation – meetings/discussion	Accessing research; internet and intranet	Travel
WEEK 1	Mon														
	Tues														
	Wed														
	Thurs														
	Fri														
WEEK 2	Mon														
	Tues														
	Wed														
	Thurs														
	Fri														

Key: Significant time ✓✓   Little time ✓   No time ✗

Key considerations about roles and tasks

- Try focusing your expectations on a 'hierarchy of need' with good induction at the bottom of the triangle as the foundation on which you will be able to build your future development.

- Manage the burden of bureaucracy by ensuring you seek out IT training as soon as possible and take time to familiarise yourself with the system and how to navigate it. It may be helpful to try to get access to the forms, reports and records of a more experienced member of staff to see how others are managing the various tasks.

- Consider what other resources could be available to you. Are there administrative or clerical staff to assist with data input or could you delegate some record-keeping to others, remembering that you will need to retain oversight and case responsibility?

- Identify the range of core tasks relevant to your own particular post and review the balance of your time use between them. Some numerical data describing an 'average week' could be really helpful in supervision, to inform discussions designed to help you maintain a mix of tasks that are satisfying for you.

Chapter 6

Time Management and the Work/Life Balance

- Organisational demands
- Time management
- Establishing a healthy work/life balance
- Key considerations for better time management and a healthy work/life balance

In this chapter we consider some of the pressures which have led to the demands that social work organisations now place on their staff, and some of the tensions that exist between the agency's expectations and your own. We take a look at how well you are using your time to meet the organisational demands placed upon you, and identify some practical strategies which might help you to feel more in control of your workload. We consider the importance of establishing and maintaining a healthy work/life balance, against a background in which many social workers feel that the normal working day is just not long enough to meet all the deadlines necessary.

Organisational demands

Social work organisations throughout the UK, and most particularly local authorities which are the main employers of social workers, are under almost constant pressure to improve their services, involving processes of change and reorganisation. The major drivers of change include the following:

- increasingly rigorous audit and inspection requirements, often resulting from the recommendations of inquiries into child abuse tragedies

- performance management targets and deadlines developed to meet the requirements of policy initiatives

- more complex funding streams and service delivery arrangements

- fewer resources accessed via ever-higher thresholds, leading to deeper, more entrenched presenting problems

- increasing public expectations of services, particularly in terms of limiting risk

- negative media representations of social work

- an increasingly litigious society, with service users and carers turning more readily to the courts.

Managerialism

Given this background, it is perhaps not surprising that social work organisations have tended to respond by embracing managerialist approaches to the delivery of their services. Marketisation and consumerism, driven by competitive tendering and 'best value' strategies, can lead to the impression that budget management and the achievement of performance targets and deadlines, rather than best practice predicated on service user need, is the agency's primary focus. All of this appears to be in direct opposition to the professional motivations and value base of many social workers, and there may be significant differences between the way in which you want to practise, and what the organisation you work for demands. These conflicting perspectives (Morrison 2001) are summarised in Table 6.1.

In response to high profile child abuse tragedies and inquiries, there is an increasing need for agencies to protect themselves against liability and blame, and systems through which practices can be ordered, standardised, recorded and audited have been developed so that there is a clear 'audit trail' from the bottom to the top of the organisation. The impression among frontline social workers subjected

Table 6.1 Comparison of practitioner and organisational perspectives
on work

Practitioner focus	Organisational approach
Process	Task
Relationship	Procedures
Outputs	Outcomes
Exploration	Rush for certainty
Mentoring	Monitoring
Depth	Surface
Change	Compliance
Context	Event
Continuity	Contract

to standardised practices and auditing, that their primary function is
to keep the organisation safe, is often inescapable.

Under pressure to collect ever-more information to meet the needs
of regulation and external inspection, the requirement for data-gath-
ering will inevitably mean an increase in the number, complexity and
frequency of agency forms that have to be completed. Organisational
systems of this sort tend to reduce any sense of personal obligation
and responsibility. Processes which focus on 'ticking boxes' are almost
certain to feel like an attempt to control your work, to limit your
autonomy and professional freedom.

Where the meaning of your work is subsumed by a tide of bureaucracy, your motivation is likely to suffer. These losses can be accentu-
ated at times by your emotional responses to the work. Depending
on the particular situations in which you become involved at work,
sadness, despair, anxiety or confusion may result, especially if you are
not able to stand back, instead becoming enmeshed in the situation.

There will inevitably be times when you feel frustration and de-
moralisation at the lack of time or resources that are available for you
to do your job. It will take time to come to your own resolution of
the conflicts inherent in the system, between your professional ideals
and the daily reality of work. As a newly qualified social worker, it is
unlikely that you will be able to influence these issues at a structural
level, at least in the immediate future, but understanding what has
driven a particular development may help you to appreciate some of
the downward pressures within the organisation. It may simply be a
salutary exercise to remember that the agency systems were developed

in response to valid pressures, and that increasing experience will mean that you are able to streamline your approaches to all of the documentation that is required of you.

Expectations of service users and carers

'Wanting to help people' is a primary motivation for most social workers, and keeping the tasks which are valued most by those who use services at the front of your mind should make an important contribution to helping you to keep a balance between your own expectations and the demands of your agency.

The research reviewed by Statham *et al.* (2006) presents a clear picture of what is valued most by service users. This includes the importance of:

- developing and maintaining respectful and listening relationships, the nature of which is central to the way in which service users perceive the quality of the services they receive

- empowering relationships, treating people as individuals and demonstrating respect by recognising what is important, and that people are experts in their own lives

- having personal qualities of honesty and reliability that inspire confidence, including not making promises that you cannot keep, and being honest about the resources available to deliver what a family wants

- being knowledgeable about local resources (as highlighted in Chapter 3) as an important part of your early introduction and orientation in the agency

- ensuring continuity, which is primarily about being able to see the same person over time (this has organisational implications for the way in which work is allocated and specialisms are divided up, as well as the retention and support of staff to minimise sickness absence and turnover)

- making time to engage with service users, who believed that social workers needed more time to develop relationships.

More specifically, when children and young people were asked about the tasks carried out by social workers that they valued most (Commission for Social Care Inspection (CSCI) 2006), the following list emerged, with the most frequently cited issues at the top:

- help with personal problems
- being listened to
- help in staying safe
- getting ready to leave care
- someone to speak on their behalf
- information following a review
- getting the right placement to live in
- contacting family
- help to keep out of trouble
- getting access to personal file
- help to cope with bullying
- getting a passport.

Given the complex and often ambiguous nature of social work, in a context of almost endemic change, the challenge lies in recognising and working with all of the tensions and how they are managed for you within the organisation. Uncertainty and anxiety cannot be eliminated altogether, but the development of individual coping mechanisms and a range of support (see Chapters 7–9), together with a satisfying organisational climate and workplace culture (see Chapter 10), are all needed if you are to maintain your morale and job satisfaction through your first year and beyond.

Time Management

The demands of social work organisations are many, and this means that social workers operate against a background in which their work is stressful, filled with interruptions and ever-changing priorities. Skill is needed to organise and manage your time so that you can be confident that what needs to be done will get done at the appropriate time. 'A day in the life of a social worker' cannot be expressed in quite the same tidy way that a teacher is able to use a timetable or a nurse a shift pattern, and this makes planning and managing time a more challenging task but one which will nevertheless produce dividends in helping you to develop a sense of control over your workload.

Social work is a busy, pressurised job, and many social workers feel that the normal working day frequently does not provide enough time in which to meet all the necessary demands. In the ebb and flow of your early professional life, working over your contract hours will be almost inevitable from time to time, and this is not in itself a bad thing. Perhaps working long hours reflects commitment but it can also mean that you miss out on personal and leisure activities, and time to relax and recover. You should remain alert to the danger of extending your working day on a regular basis, and seeing these additional hours as a mark of dedication, because in all probability your efforts will go unnoticed and are likely to be unappreciated.

Making more effective use of your work time by prioritising tasks should mean that the times when work needs to spill over into your personal, family or leisure time are kept to a minimum.

Time use survey

Managing time effectively requires you to take a realistic view about how much you can do and what you can reasonably expect of yourself, and then to plan ahead to meet the priorities. Completing the questionnaire in Box 6.1 may help you to identify the areas where you can make some efficiency savings.

Time management strategies

There are a number of guiding principles for good time management which should help you to make efficient use of your time at work. These include:

- planning ahead

- being clear about what you need to get done

- being aware of when potential problems, such as interruptions or your own habits, will make things difficult

- knowing when you can be flexible and when you cannot

- having strategies for coping with problems when they occur

- not making extra work by being disorganised.

Box 6.1 Time use questionnaire

How efficiently do you use your time?

For each statement, choose the option which most closely reflects the way you work by putting a tick in one box in each row. The aim of the exercise is to mark everything as 'always'. If you have options marked in the other columns:

- Which of them could you move at least one column to the left?
- What do you need to change in order to make the move?

	Always	Usually	Sometimes	Rarely
I make and use a weekly plan				
I create blocks of time for big jobs				
I deal with interruptions effectively				
I deal with paperwork effectively				
I can find what I need easily on my desk				
I can find what I need easily in the recording system				
I can find what I need easily on the intranet				
Discussions with colleagues are to the point				
Team meetings are short and focused				
I delegate where possible and use others well				
My manager seems to respect my time				
I plan my leisure activities and stick to them				
I find time to relax outside work				
I feel in control of my working day				

Source: adapted from Thody, Gray and Bowden (2000)

The checklist in Box 6.2 is designed to help you identify the 'pinch points' in your everyday work, where the workload mounts up and might threaten to overwhelm you.

Box 6.2 Time and tasks: checklist

Identify the routine things that you do every day:

- Do your feelings change with different tasks?

- Are there certain times of day when you are more tired or less motivated?

- Do you allocate an amount of time to specific activities?

- How often do you spend just the allocated time on an activity? How often do you go over?

- What are your main time-wasters, e.g. interruptions, chatting, looking for something?

- What avoidance routines do you indulge in?

Source: adapted from Siviter (2008)

PRIORITISING

Organising your workload means that you will need to set priorities, identifying those tasks that need to be done now and those that can safely wait until later. Using a filtering system to sort your work into daily, weekly and monthly deadlines is a good start in getting organised. For example, individual tasks can be grouped together into one of four categories:

1. *Essential*: to be done before anything else

2. *Important*: better done sooner rather than later

3. *Routine*: can wait until later

4. *Interest*: for future reference.

Setting deadlines for important pieces of work is essential. Commit to a particular date, marked in your diary, which in good times acts as a reminder to keep you on track and in adversity will prompt you to review and reschedule your workload, according to new priorities and pressures.

TAKING CONTROL OF PAPERWORK AND EMAILS

To prevent the accumulation of a paper mountain on your desk, or a long list of emails on your computer, it is important to sort out this material on a routine basis. Do not give each piece of paper or electronic message equal 'weight' or value. Instead, divide them into items which can simply be jettisoned, generally those that are of no direct relevance or use to you; those needing a quick or concise response that can be dealt with straightaway; and those that are important and need your detailed attention. As a general 'rule', try to handle each piece of paper or electronic message once only.

DELEGATING

It is almost certain that, at times, you will have too much to do. One person often cannot do everything, and delegating or sharing your work with others is an integral part of professional practice. Amidst all the competing pressures and demands on your time, it is important to be able to separate out the tasks that can be done only by you, and those that others might do safely and appropriately. You may think of delegation as one of the more challenging tasks for a new member of the team but asking yourself some of the following questions when you are thinking about delegating a task to someone else could help to highlight any difficulties or pitfalls:

- What can only a qualified member of staff do? What are the legal constraints and agency policy?

- Does the task require professional judgement or skilled social work intervention?

- Is there someone else with the necessary knowledge and skills to whom I might delegate and, if so, what support will they need?

- If I do delegate a task, what would be the worst thing that could go wrong?

- Is there any reason I should not delegate the task? Am I just being lazy?

- What is the best use of my time in the interests of service users and carers?

INTERRUPTIONS

Interruptions can have a negative impact on your efficiency. If they come from service users, there may be little that you can do about them. But interruptions can also come from inside and outside the office, from colleagues or other professionals. There are a number of ways of responding to these, but you must ensure that you do not become a victim of the pincer movement between a busy job and other people's needs. You must balance your needs with those of your colleagues, and learn not to feel guilty about prioritising your own needs.

HELP WITH SAYING 'NO'

Saying 'No' may well be one of the most important skills in a busy, pressurised workplace. There is a real temptation when you are new to 'prove' your enthusiasm and commitment by accepting every task offered to you. However, ultimately this is not likely to be helpful, either to you or others. You can be professional and collegiate and still keep the demands on your time within reasonable limits. If you feel that you need help to say 'No', the following might prove a useful strategy:

- Delay the decision – request time to think about it.

- Offer some support but opt out of taking on the full load.

- Say that you would like to help but that you have to work on other priority tasks at the moment.

- Propose an alternative arrangement that you think is manageable for you.

Establishing a healthy work/life balance

Newly qualified social workers can struggle, at times, to manage the duality of their role: balancing personal involvement in people's lives with the ability to stand back, make judgements and reach often hard decisions. You may find that it is difficult to leave your cases and concerns for service users behind at the end of the working day, allowing feelings of anxiety to percolate from work into your personal life, giving rise to increased levels of stress. This can be amplified for those who perhaps live alone, whose partners are working abroad, or who have caring responsibilities for young children. The extra burden of stress brought into the workplace by those in caring professions, who also have other caring responsibilities at home, but who are unsupported to carry out the emotional work involved in their family situations, has been reported by Wharton and Erickson (1995), and our own findings show a close correlation with those outcomes. There is also some evidence that balancing the different sources of stress has a particularly negative effect on job satisfaction for women. As the vast majority of social workers are women these findings might be considered particularly pertinent.

Feelings of stress and anxiety are no surprise to those joining a new profession, and understanding, help and support will be needed to enable you to establish an appropriate work/life balance if you are not to feel overwhelmed. The rebalancing mechanisms have been more fully reported in relation to other professions, such as nursing (Gerrish 2005; Maben and Macleod Clark 1998; Mooney 2007) and teaching (Parkinson and Pritchard 2005), but rather different pressures and working practices seem to apply to the newly qualified staff in these occupations. For example, nurses do not bear case responsibility for individual patients in quite the same way as social workers and, to some extent, the wearing and removing of a uniform, coupled with the handover to another team at the end of each shift, defrays some of the burden in a way not usually available to social workers. And for teachers, since the introduction in 1999 of a probationary year, a workload reduction has been obligatory for the first 12 months, and all qualified teachers are provided with time away from the classroom (non-contact time) for planning and assessment. As we have already noted, teachers are also not expected to carry out a range of specified clerical duties, including data input.

The pilot programmes being introduced for newly qualified staff working in children's services should help to reduce some of the demands and increase the support available to NQSWs in their first year of employment. However, the present arrangements are relatively limited in scope, and it will still be helpful for you to monitor your time and tasks for discussion with your line manager in supervision.

Achieving an appropriate balance

Growing evidence shows that people who work extended hours actually end up producing less, rather than more. Achieving a healthy work/life balance means different things to different people, but it is important to achieve a balance which means that you are working to have a satisfying and healthy life, rather than simply living to work. Proper sleep, a balanced diet and physical exercise all have a part to play in minimising the negative effects of a stressful job. Maintain a healthy separation between work and home by confining your work to the office. Practise working only within your designated hours, and try to eliminate or at least minimise the occasions on which you take work home. This is a very important boundary which should not be breached lightly.

Preserving breaks and leave

As a general rule, you should take your daily lunch break. The way you spend your break can also serve either to energise you or to sap your strength. Getting outside for a short walk can improve your sense of well-being, and chatting with positive people, not malcontents, can nourish a good mood.

It is also important to make sure that you preserve your annual leave, days off and study days. Try to use the time available to you at weekends and during holidays to focus on yourself and your family. Well-planned relaxation and time to pursue your own interests will mean that you can return to work refreshed.

Key considerations for better time management and a healthy work/life balance

- Effective time management is primarily about getting organised, setting priorities and having a system which will allow you to track progress and review deadlines.

- Plan ahead – setting daily, weekly and monthly deadlines can be helpful.

- Be clear about priorities – group your tasks into one of four categories: essential/important/routine/interest.

- Working over your contract hours will be almost inevitable from time to time and this is not in itself a bad thing.

- Be aware of the danger of extending your working day on a regular basis: the additional hours are unlikely to be noticed or appreciated in the way you might like or expect.

- Try to resist the very real and understandable temptation when you are new to 'prove' your enthusiasm and commitment by accepting every task offered to you – learn how to say 'No'.

Part III

Jumping the Hurdles

Part III focuses on the period after induction as you take on an increasing workload and begin to deal with some of the stresses as well as the pleasures of the job. We explore ways of finding support from a wide range of sources, including the team and a two-way 'supervisory alliance', as well as positive coping strategies for working in stressful situations.

Stress is not always a bad thing. Some degree of stress *can* be good for you in providing motivation to achieve things which you might have thought were out of reach. Chapter 7 'Dealing with Stress, Emotion and Exhaustion' explores a range of demands, constraints and personal traits affecting workplace stress and job satisfaction as well as identifying helpful strategies and positive coping mechanisms. It is important to realise that the support you need cannot be found in one place and Chapter 8 'Finding Support' considers access to a range of different sources and types of support, to meet your needs in different situations and at different times, as an essential requirement for all social workers. Although it may feel imperative to prioritise tasks focused on service user needs, there is an equal imperative to take time to consider and prioritise your own needs.

Chapter 9 'Taking Part in Supervision' is devoted entirely to supervision: its three participants and functions, its central place in providing support and guidance for all social workers, and the importance of your active participation, in leading the agenda and preparing fully for each session. You need to remain mindful of the fact that even supervision – on its own – has its limits and if the work demands being placed on you are too great, the need to take positive action is unavoidable.

Chapter 7

Dealing with Stress, Emotion and Exhaustion

• Identifying stressors

• Negative consequences of stress

• Coping mechanisms

• Key considerations in dealing with stress, emotion and exhaustion

Stress is experienced subjectively, with individuals reacting in very different ways to the same situation (Storey and Billingham 2001). While a certain amount of stress can be good for you, too much can produce tension, anxiety and depression. As the following quotes illustrate, stress has been recognised as a serious problem in the workplace for many years:

> Overwork can kill ... especially if combined with high demand, low control and poor social support ... job strain predicted mortality. (Michie and Cockcroft 1996, p.921)

> Stress is still the biggest problem in UK workplaces with excessive workloads, job cuts and rapid change the most common triggers for rising stress levels among employees ... stress is the greatest cause of absence from work. (Trades Union Congress 2006)

Numerous studies and reports have concluded that social work is an extremely demanding job. As far back as 1980, Maslach demonstrated that factors intrinsic to the job, rather than the personality of those engaged in doing it, are highly related to burnout (Maslach 1980).

Managing stress at work therefore needs to begin with a clear acknowledgement that stress is an organisational concern rather than an individual failing (Thompson *et al.* 1996).

There is more about the effects of organisational culture on social workers in Chapter 10, but in this chapter we focus in more detail on what causes stress and the steps you can take to deal with its negative consequences by developing effective coping mechanisms.

Identifying stressors

To help you make sense of some of the ideas in this chapter, and to apply them to your own work situation, you might find it helpful to answer the questions in Box 7.1 before reading the rest of the chapter.

Box 7.1 How do you work with stressful situations?

Part 1: Identifying stressors

Call to mind a challenging situation you have dealt with at work involving service users, managers, colleagues or other professionals. Jot down some of your thoughts in answer to the following questions:

- What happened?

- What were the most upsetting aspects?

- What impact did the experience have on you at the time?

- What were the longer term effects of the experience?

Stress occurs when there is a lack of balance in the demands and constraints placed on a person in relation to the internal and external supports available to them (Jones, Fletcher and Ibbetson 1991). This definition is helpful in three ways: first, because it introduces the important idea of bringing competing demands into some sort of balance; second, because it emphasises that stress is not a static state but a dynamic one involving three key elements – demands, constraints and support; and third, because it makes reference to 'internal supports', alerting us to the role of personal characteristics.

Several disciplines have developed models of stress but, as in the ecological model of social work with children and families (Jack

1997), it is those which reflect the dynamic interrelationship of a range of different factors that are most helpful in trying to understand occupational or work-related stress in social work (Karasek 1979; Lazarus and Folkman 1984). The domains affecting workplace stress and job satisfaction – demands, constraints and personal traits – are presented in Figure 7.1 along each of the three sides of a triangle, enabling the interactions between different factors within each domain, particular to social work, to be analysed.

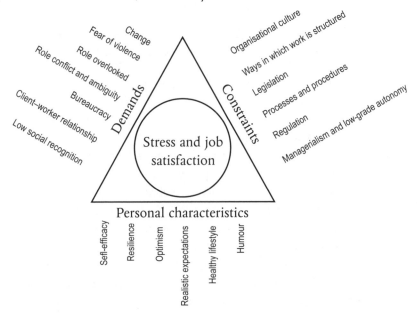

Figure 7.1 The interaction of demands, constraints and personal characteristics in stress and job satisfaction

A large number of studies have shown that high demands in a job may not be stressful if there are low constraints, good levels of support and high levels of control and autonomy (Bennett, Evans and Tattersall 1993; Collins 2007; Jenaro, Flores and Arias 2007; Jones *et al.* 1991; Morris 2005; Rogers 2001; Sargent and Terry 2000; Smith and Nursten 1998; Storey and Billingham 2001). Increased support and self-efficacy help to reduce feelings of stress, even though the demands of the job may be high.

Demands

The factors presented along this side of the triangle are all frequently identified demands of the job, which can provoke feelings of stress, anxiety and exhaustion. Newly qualified social workers are often surprised and even shocked by the demands of their first employment following qualification.

❝ This is so different from the job I expected. This isn't what I was trained to do at all. (NQSW)

I still wake up sometimes at 2 am in the morning and start thinking about cases, worrying about stuff, did I do this, should I have done that, if I'd done this differently would that have had a better outcome, especially with cases that I don't feel completely at ease about. (NQSW) **❞**

In response to frequent policy developments and new government initiatives, social work agencies nowadays are engaged in an almost continual process of *change*. Opportunities abound, but not without a good deal of uncertainty, which is well documented as a source of workplace stress. This means that skills in managing change are becoming almost core requirements for anyone entering the social work profession. Actual or threatened *violence* is another important cause of stress in the everyday working lives of social workers (Smith and Nursten 1998), with particular implications here for lone working. Following the Baby Peter case in Haringey, a Unison '10-point plan' (UNISON 2008) called for all child protection investigation visits to be conducted by two practitioners, each with at least two years' post-qualifying experience.

Overload refers to feelings of being overwhelmed – either by having too much to do and too little time in which to do it, or by the allocation of tasks which are beyond your present level of confidence, ability or training. Research into the new qualifying degrees (Social Care Workforce Research Unit (SCWRU) 2008) found that it was common practice to allocate large numbers of child protection cases to newly qualified social workers, a practice which was also reported as a common experience by the NQSWs.

" And you know, when you're carrying a caseload of 18, 20, 22, I would just cancel supervision just to get work done. (NQSW)

And I mean at my highest, I was carrying 22 when I was newly qualified with 8 of those being child protection. (Social worker, 9 months post-qualification) **"**

While the Social Care Council in England has called for the introduction of national guidelines on minimum staffing requirements based on an agreed workload model (Community Care 2008), until these emerge it is important for you to raise any serious concerns that you have about workload issues in supervision, as well as more broadly within the team in which you are working. Help in saying 'No' (Chapter 6) could be useful in this regard.

Role conflict and ambiguity arise in circumstances where your own beliefs and values are either incompatible with those of the organisation, or where there are unclear boundaries and lines of accountability in relation to your duties and responsibilities. Where these issues exist they may also need to be discussed in supervision, or with members of the team in which you are working. *Bureaucracy* is often experienced as a rising tide of paperwork, complex forms, problematic IT systems and performance management processes. These have become persistent sources of pressure, frustration and stress for many social workers (see Chapter 5 for more on dealing with the bureaucratic burden).

The sensitivity and responsiveness needed to deal with the difficult range of problems that can be presented by *client–worker relationships* potentially exposes social workers to particularly stressful situations, and it has been noted that those working with children and families are sometimes less able to distance themselves and are more likely to become enmeshed in the concerns of the service users with whom they are working (Bennett *et al.* 1993). For example, restricted resources often lead to perceptions of having made an inadequate response to service user need, because the only choices for action appear to be between a number of equally unsatisfactory alternatives. This can combine with the *low social recognition* and poor regard for the profession which are frequently identified by social workers as another source of stress. In particular, following child abuse tragedies, media portrayals and political criticisms of social work incompetence lead to feelings of being undervalued and misunderstood compared with other professionals working with children and young people.

Constraints

Factors which limit or constrain the autonomy and decision-making of social workers are gathered together along the right-hand side of the triangle. The *culture of the organisation* in which you operate is perhaps the most significant constraining influence. The layers of responsibility within an organisational structure can serve to frustrate attempts to make speedy, sensible decisions at the frontline, and when decisions have been made, a 'blame culture' can leave you feeling isolated and alone when problems arise.

The *ways in which work is structured* can also present significant constraints on your practice (Stevenson 1981). For example, current trends towards a greater number of 'specialist' teams and the contracting out of services can result in unhelpful fragmentation of knowledge, skills and resources. Despite the fact that children and young people cite frequent changes of social worker as one of their main concerns (Morgan 2006), organisational imperatives often mean that you have little control over the nature and length of your contact with service users. The associated lack of continuity is likely to have a detrimental effect, not only on the child or young person concerned, but also on your own sense of achievement and self-efficacy.

Legislation and *regulation* also present major external constraints on your practice, often limiting individual creativity and professional autonomy. For example, all social work agencies are regulated and have to be accountable for their performance, which requires that ever-increasing amounts of data are collected, often using tick-box forms that have to be completed by practitioners and managers within set deadlines. *Managerialism* has flourished in such a climate, with bureaucratic approaches to the allocation and measurement of workloads, for example, having taken hold across almost all social work organisations. While most social workers recognise the pressures on first line managers to set and meet performance targets, it has been shown that the pressure involved in planning and meeting these kinds of deadlines is a strong predictor of overall stress for those in frontline services (Morris 2005).

Personal characteristics

Clearly, some of the demands and constraints considered above will be more readily amenable to individual control than others, so we now go on to consider the personal characteristics which have been shown to have a moderating effect on the experience of occupational stress.

Self-efficacy, which in this context is the belief in your own capability to organise and carry out a course of action to successfully perform your job, is one of the variables which plays an important part in the relationship between demands, constraints and job satisfaction. For example, there is evidence of a direct relationship between high levels of self-efficacy and increased learning, persistence and job performance in complex situations (Jimmieson 2000). *Resilience* also plays a part in determining how individual workers respond to different experiences. However, it needs to be recognised that resilience is not a static characteristic, and will be influenced by the context and the culture of the organisation in which you are working, which can facilitate or hinder the development of your ability to bounce back from negative emotional experiences. While many social work methods are based on the central importance of relationships and emotion, it is somewhat ironic that many social workers are expected to undertake their work in bureaucratic organisations, driven by structures, procedures and rules which effectively ignore personal emotion, and treat staff more or less as 'technical operatives', with little professional freedom, autonomy and choice in decision-making.

Optimism is another important characteristic that makes a healthy contribution to the ability to bounce back and sustain a positive psychological state and good self-esteem. It may either be expressed as a global expectation that good things will be plentiful in the future and bad things scarce, or as an explanatory style which blames external factors for bad events, identifying specific causes and how these might be changed. By contrast, the explanatory style of a pessimist will favour internal, long-lasting and all-pervasive personal causes which cannot be changed (Collins 2007). These concepts lean heavily on the early work of Seligman (1975) on learned helplessness, which proposed that after experiencing uncontrollable events people become unresponsive and passive through a learned general expectancy that future outcomes will be unrelated to any of their own actions. It may be worth noting that Seligman (2006) later reframed these explanatory styles in terms of 'learned optimism', based on the ability to frame stressful situations as challenges offering potential benefits and opportunities. However, it is also important to retain *realistic expectations*. Taking a relentlessly optimistic approach can lead you into pursuing unachievable goals, or striving for control over events without taking proper account of the constraints involved. Optimism must therefore be used as a flexible response, in appropriate circumstances, rather than as a habitual reflex, regardless of context. The greatest value of optimism is that it encourages a search for possibilities, positives and strengths, all of which should underpin your work with service users.

As discussed in Chapter 6, a *healthy lifestyle*, particularly involving exercise, can also be an effective means of coping and improving stress management, while an unhealthy lifestyle can increase the negative effects of workplace stress. Although it has been noted that those (especially women) constrained by other demands, such as family care-giving activities, are more likely to have less energy and time to exercise (Burton and Turrell 2000), in 2005 a study in Finland found that women employed in the public sector who took more physical exercise were more satisfied with combining their job and family responsibilities (Kouvonen *et al.* 2005).

The final personal characteristic considered along the bottom of the triangle is *a sense of humour*. Cited as a requirement in so many recruitment advertisements, humour applied to social work can be a controversial topic. The sensitivity of a particular situation may not call for humour, and sometimes there may simply be no funny side to things. However, it has been shown that a sense of humour can mitigate the effects of stress, producing the same kinds of calm, positive well-being and health benefits known to be associated with exercise and relaxation (Martin 2001). For example, in a study involving focus group discussions with informal carers conducted by one of the authors, participants frequently commented on the value of 'being able to laugh' in the face of difficult and challenging situations, providing a release for emotion that might otherwise be unbearable. Laughing at one's own difficult situations in this way, often referred to as 'gallows humour', seems to bring a sense of control to situations which are largely uncontrollable, and is self-affirming as well as promoting bonding and support, as it did for these carers. In this context, it is interesting to note that a study of social work students (Moran and Hughes 2006) found that they scored lower than average for their sense of humour, which may indicate that encouragement and 'permission' from supervisors and managers to use humour as an appropriate coping mechanism may be needed before social workers feel free to draw on its potential benefits.

Negative consequences of stress

While stress does not result in serious ill-health for most, the 'ripple effect' on others in the workplace, and on the work or service offered, can be considerable, especially over time. We noted at the beginning of this chapter that an optimum level of stress can be good for you, acting as a positive motivational incentive to achieve things that might not otherwise be possible. Stress becomes dangerous, however, when there is a loss of balance between what is being demanded of you and the resources available to you to achieve it, and can result in poor decision-making, presenteeism or absenteeism, and burnout.

Poor decision-making

When stress is too challenging, rather than enjoying and developing through your work experiences, just surviving them becomes the major imperative, and your usual behaviour may begin to alter. You might experience any (or all) of the following:

- loss of concentration

- an inability to handle new information

- an increased tendency to procrastinate or postpone activities

- hasty decision-making or 'panicked' choices

- oversimplification of alternatives

- a reduction in creative thinking

- more defensiveness about your decisions

- more irrational or hostile feelings

- increasing withdrawal and social isolation.

In these circumstances, as reported by Morris (2005), the quality of decision-making becomes diminished and more 'risky', with potentially serious implications. There is growing evidence of an inability to handle new information and to hold a more defensive decision position among stressed social workers. For example, a Canadian study of child protection service workers found that, among those who decided there was no risk to the child in a case of chronic neglect, higher stress scores predicted making this decision early and holding it with greater certainty (McGee 1989).

Presenteeism and absenteeism

'Presenteeism' (Wikipedia 2001), a word coined in 2001 by Cary Cooper, Professor of Organisational Psychology and Health at Manchester University, refers to the inappropriate non-use of sick leave, which is a growing concern in many workplaces where it is associated with increasing levels of stress. It can be difficult to disclose stress in an organisational culture where it is viewed as a sign of individual weakness. Fear of blame, a misplaced commitment to service users and colleagues, or jeopardising progression and promotion by having a poor attendance record sometimes seem compelling reasons to remain at work when really you should be at home because of illness. Where 'presenteeism' exists, short-term absences may well be low, but longer absences may increase due to the eventual onset of more serious physical or psychological illness. The irony, here, is that working in an organisation beset by longer-term *absenteeism* actually increases the stresses experienced by those remaining at work, leading to yet more absences and associated difficulties with staff recruitment and retention. In these circumstances your morale, as well as arrangements for your ongoing supervision, support and development, are bound to be jeopardised. Before applying for or accepting a new post, it could be worth looking at vacancy rates (which are published by the Department for Children, Schools and Families, and can be found on some organisations' websites) to get an understanding of which employers are performing better in this regard.

Burnout

Burnout is the final consequence of chronic, unalleviated work stress, and studies have shown that there is a high incidence of burnout in professionals who provide care to children at risk (McGee 1989). The risks and perils of burnout should not be underestimated, and you would do well to remain vigilant on your own behalf, as well as for colleagues. Burnout combines feelings of emotional exhaustion with negative attitudes towards the organisation and colleagues and depersonalisation towards service users (Maslach and Leiter 1997).

Figure 7.2 (adapted from Karasek 1979) summarises the major conditions for burnout, in terms of the balance between the demands of your job and the level of control you feel you have (four quadrants), as well as the associated impacts on professional development and job satisfaction (oblong boxes). On each side of the circle, a level of support, either high or low, has been added to the critical factors influencing positive development or burnout. Since individual variables, such as coping strategies and job satisfaction, account for only 20 per cent of the symptoms of burnout (Jenaro *et al.* 2007), careful attention needs to be paid to external factors. The single most important 'buffer' against stress and burnout cited by social workers, not only in our own research but also in a number of other studies (Bednar 2003; Collins 2007; Stalker *et al.* 2007; Tadeka *et al.* 2005), is seeking and finding support, from a wide range of sources, which is the focus of Chapter 8.

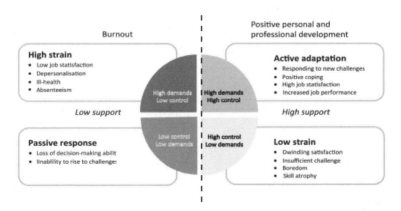

Figure 7.2 Conditions for burnout

Coping mechanisms

At the beginning of this chapter we identified that stress is an almost inevitable aspect of social work, arising from the interplay between personal, structural and organisational factors intrinsic to the job. So how do you cope – modifying and adapting your behaviour to meet the demands of the job? See Box 7.2.

Box 7.2 How do you work with stressful situations?

Part 2: Using internal and external resources

Reflect in a bit more depth on your experiences of the situation that you identified at the beginning of the chapter:

- What coping mechanisms, if any, did you employ to deal with the stresses you encountered?

- What influenced your choice?

- Did you consider any alternative strategies?

Coping mechanisms are crucial in helping you to deal with stressful situations at work. Coping can involve either taking action when something constructive can be done to alter the cause of the stress (i.e. problem focused), or it can be aimed at reducing or managing the distress you are experiencing when the cause of the stress is outside your control (i.e. emotion focused). It is instructive to look at some unhelpful responses first, before going on to consider a range of helpful coping strategies.

Unhelpful strategies

There are a number of largely unhelpful ways of trying to deal with stress at work. Among the most common are the four 'Ds' – diversion, disengagement, denial and depersonalisation.

Diversion involves directing attention elsewhere, for instance by inappropriate use of sick leave or even handing in an abrupt resignation.

Disengagement can take one of two forms. The first, known as behavioural disengagement or self-blaming, involves marginalising the part that you feel you can play in determining your circumstances, thereby reducing your efforts and effectively giving up. This attitude has close links with the 'learned helplessness' described by Seligman (1975). The other form is mental disengagement, which involves escape or avoidance. This takes over when you distance yourself from thinking about behavioural responses to a demanding situation. It may present itself in a range of activities such as wishful thinking, day-dreaming, excessive sleeping, or the misuse of alcohol and drugs.

Denial is a form of coping involving a refusal to believe that a stressor exists. It has links with pessimism, and an excessive focus on emotional distress and disengagement. Rather worryingly, a study of coping styles by Fineman (1985) found that the internalisation of difficulties, allowing them to build up in the hope that they will disappear or be released elsewhere, was the most dominant coping style used by social workers at that time.

Depersonalisation can be thought of as a coping strategy that is neither problem focused nor emotion focused. Depersonalisation is characterised by negative, cynical or impersonal feelings towards those who use services, and is often the ultimate response of someone working in an environment which they perceive as hostile, when all other strategies do not seem to work any longer. It is used to avoid experiencing severe levels of emotional exhaustion, and can be a forerunner of more serious burnout.

Helpful strategies

More helpful coping strategies include acceptance, balanced expectations, positive reappraisal, rehearsal, the ventilation of feelings, self-detachment, and a range of problem-focused strategies.

As a rule of thumb in dealing with stress, it is usually helpful to start with the most straightforward approach, and if you can accept the reality of a situation then you have already put yourself in the best position to resolve it. *Acceptance* is a functional coping response where the source of stress cannot be easily changed and you are able to recognise that it will need to be accommodated in some way. The general message, here, is that you should not attempt to control the uncontrollable – if a stressor cannot be changed, you can retain a sense of control by changing your expectations and attitudes, looking for the positive side of a situation, and accepting that the world is rarely perfect and that people make mistakes. Job satisfaction also tends to be enhanced when your work-related thinking combines both optimistic and pessimistic perceptions into *balanced expectations*. Positive or engaged coping mechanisms often have their roots in finding a balance between a hopeful interpretation of the situation and a realistic appreciation of its difficulties or stressors, with awareness of the possibilities for progress or change coexisting alongside an acknowledgement of the constraints.

You can also apply techniques with which you will already be familiar from the field of cognitive behavioural therapy (CBT). For example, *positive reappraisal* is a type of emotion-focused coping aimed at managing distress. Talking about emotions and feelings can help to put stressful circumstances into a broader or wider perspective, so that you see them in a more favourable light. This might involve making a positive social comparison with others in a worse position, reappraising a situation as one which could happen to anyone, or using humour appropriately. 'Stress inoculation' is another CBT approach that you can use to cope when you are feeling stressed. By consciously giving yourself time to plan, you can prepare yourself for a difficult or challenging situation, *rehearsing* a number of possible responses in advance, for example in a learning set or supervision session.

In the early stages of dealing with a stressful situation, it may also be helpful to seek opportunities to *ventilate your feelings*, avoiding 'catastrophising' demanding events by expressing your feelings, rather than letting them build up inside. Failing to voice feelings, in an open, honest and respectful manner, often means that the situation has no chance to improve and is more likely to deteriorate. However, this approach is probably best employed on a restricted basis, as overuse for prolonged periods can impede adjustment, distracting you from active coping and moving on to more positive reappraisal. Increased levels of *self-detachment* have also been shown to protect against emotional exhaustion in social work (Ying 2008). This type of coping is fostered by making efforts to stand back from your experiences, so that you are protected against an over-identification with subjective emotions. It also involves recognising that what you perceive as your own shortcomings or difficulties are often part of the wider human condition, experienced by almost everyone at some time in their lives, and that you therefore need to employ a measure of forgiveness in relation to your own shortcomings, rather than harsh, critical judgement and self-blame.

Finally, positive *problem-focused strategies*, involving active engagement in thinking about how to cope with a stressor – gathering information and coming up with what practical steps to take – can be employed. Even in apparently uncontrollable or deteriorating situations, it is possible to identify goals, and experience efficacy, mastery and control in working towards them. Problem-focused coping helps to focus your attention, and has clear parallels with your existing knowledge, skills and understanding of task-centred practice. By approaching a difficulty or stressor in this way, you will be nurturing positive feelings of your effectiveness and control, both of which have been shown to be critical elements in maintaining positive well-being (Collins 2007). This type of coping is fostered by identifying your priorities, putting other activities aside in order to focus without distraction on a particular stressor, consciously putting time and space between yourself and a stressor to avoid acting prematurely, setting standards that are reasonable, and learning to be content with some things that are 'good enough'. Trying to be perfect is a major source of avoidable stress, and taking time to reflect on the positive things in your life, including your personal abilities, talents and interests away from work, is likely to be beneficial.

Finally, returning to the exercise that has run throughout the chapter, there is an opportunity now to reflect on your own coping mechanisms, and how you might work more effectively with stressful situations in the future. See Box 7.3.

Box 7.3 How do you work with stressful situations?

Part 3: Coping mechanisms

Reflect further on the work situation that you identified for this exercise at the beginning of the chapter:

- What was the outcome of your coping response?

- How satisfied were you with it?

- Are there any alternative coping strategies that could help you improve your responses and the outcome in a similar situation in future?

Key considerations in dealing with stress, emotion and exhaustion

- Stress *can* be good for you. Some degree of stress can be a positive, motivational incentive to achieve things that otherwise might not have been possible.

- Balance is an important issue in dealing with stress. Positive coping is rooted in striking a balance between a hopeful interpretation of a situation and a realistic appraisal of its difficulties or constraints.

- Demands, constraints and personal traits are the three key elements affecting workplace stress and job satisfaction. Identifying the critical factors (along each side of the triangle) particular to your own situation might provide you with an early warning of any imbalance developing between them, and trigger a timely look at your coping strategies.

- Helpful strategies to be nurtured and fostered are those that are either problem focused, aimed at reducing or removing entirely whatever has caused the stress, or emotion focused, where the cause of the stress lies outside your control and reducing the distress is your aim.

- Trying to control the uncontrollable will put you in an impossible position. Recognising and separating what you can affect from that which is beyond your control will make a really positive contribution to your psychological well-being.

Chapter 8

Finding Support

- : Mapping your support networks
- : Personal resources
- : Support from others
- : Organisational support
- : Key considerations in finding support

This chapter aims to identify the specific support needs of newly qualified social workers, exploring the structure of teams and their place in providing personal and professional support, together with the role of wider social support networks, both inside and outside the organisation.

Support has three main functions, each linked to the coping mechanisms discussed in Chapter 7. At a very basic level, support can take the form of practical advice and information, as part of problem-focused coping, which involves gathering information and identifying practical options. Support can also be a part of emotion-focused coping, when there is a need for help with your feelings in facing a difficult situation or dealing with its aftermath. The third function is to support healthy emotional adjustment, facilitated by talking, which can help you to cope with stress. Disclosure of stressful events and talking about the emotions associated with them is more likely to lead to positive readjustment when there are supportive networks (Lepore, Ragan and Jones 2000).

Studies looking specifically at social work (Stalker *et al.* 2007; Tadeka *et al.* 2005) have shown the importance of having a *range* of different sources of support available, at different times, for newly qualified staff as they move through induction, transition and beyond.

An early theme to emerge from our own interviews with newly qualified social workers (see Table 8.1 later in the chapter) is the central importance of the people who are part of your team, networks and management structures, in helping you to settle in and develop confident and competent practice during your first 12 months in post, and you should ensure that you make the best of every opportunity to build relationships and networks both inside and outside your organisation. Support in all its guises – from your own personal resources, from others, at home and at work, both formal and informal – will help you to balance the oscillating levels of stress which are an almost intrinsic part of the job. The relationship is represented diagrammatically in Figure 8.1.

Figure 8.1 Relationship between workplace stress and support

Mapping your support networks

You are probably familiar with eco-mapping as a way of making an assessment of a family's social relationships when you are working with service users, but you can apply this approach to your own circumstances as well. It can provide a dynamic overview of your circumstances, highlighting important connections and sources of support (as well as deficits and barriers) essential for your well-being, both now and into the future. According to Warren (1993), an eco-map is

> an ecological metaphor [that] can lead social workers to see the client not as an isolated entity for study, but as a part of a complex ecological system. Such a view helps them to focus on the sources of nurturance, stimulation and support that must be available in the intimate and extended environment to make possible growth and survival. (Warren 1993, p.40)

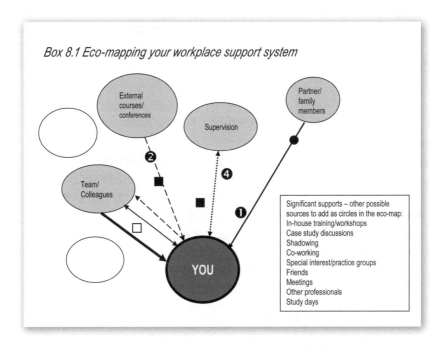

Box 8.1 Eco-mapping your workplace support system

To complete your own eco-map, you first need to identify the people or resources that are significant in supporting your learning and development, and some examples are suggested in Box 8.1. Personalise this by filling in the blank circles and removing or adding new ones, as necessary. Draw lines to each circle to make the connections that exist in your network, describing those relationships by:

Using different lines to indicate the nature of the relationship, for example:

Practical; _____ Emotional; _ _ _ _ Information/Advice; ......
Critical.......

Adding a number (or a different colour) for the quality of the support, for example:

1 = strong; 2 = tenuous; 3 = distant; 4 = stressful; 5 = non-existent

Putting arrows on each line to signify the direction of help (or stress); for example:

flow both ways ⟷; flow to you ←; flow from you →

Adding a symbol for how frequently you call on that support; for example:

● Daily; □ Weekly; ■ Monthly; ◆ Few times per year

However creatively (or not!) you are able to complete the exercise, the real strength of any eco-map lies in its simple, visual impact. It not only collects and organises a great deal of factual information but also displays, all on one side of A4 paper, the relationships between the important variables so that connections, themes and qualities are all brought into sharp focus for you.

Once you have it completed, use your eco-map to help you consider some of the following questions:

- Am I getting the sort of support I need?

- What is missing? What can I do to bridge any gaps?

- Which sources of support do I find most helpful and unhelpful?

- What actions can I take to foster and maintain them or reduce their impact?

- Which areas need strengthening? What action can I take to build up my network?

Personal resources

Job crafting

As we have already noted in Chapter 5, finding meaning in doing a worthwhile job plays a central role for many in making the choice of social work as a career, and finding significance and a sense of purpose in your work can also help you to deal with its stresses. There is evidence that even in the most restricted jobs employees can exert some influence over job boundaries and tasks to achieve a more positive sense of meaning and self-worth in their work. This has been called 'job crafting' (Wrzesniewski and Dutton 2001), which recognises the importance of personal control over even seemingly small matters. By taking control of or reframing some of the tasks, conditions or purposes of the work, 'job crafters' are able to make the job their own, creating new possibilities for self-accomplishment and mastery. Job identities are never fully determined by formal job descriptions, and resourceful job crafters will seek out the areas of latitude to actively reshape the tasks and social relationships of their role in a way that enables a more positive sense of self to be expressed and confirmed by others. Fostering this kind of mindset might relieve, for instance, some of the weight of bureaucracy which so often threatens to eclipse much of the day-to-day satisfaction in the social work role.

Making use of positive emotions

Positive emotions can also help to reduce levels of stress by 'quieting or undoing' negative emotions. Primary appraisal of a stressful situation offers you the opportunity to interpret it as one in which there is the possibility for change and gain, stimulating positive emotions such as eagerness, confidence, happiness and pride. In a Community Care survey in 2006, 90 per cent of social workers reported feeling a sense of pride in their work. These states of stress can be differentiated along a continuum as shown in Figure 8.2.

| Distress/ chaos | ⟷ | Anxiety/ stress | ⟷ | Eagerness/ excitement | ⟷ | Happiness/ pride |

Figure 8.2 The stress continuum

Positive emotions are just as much a part of managing stress as negative ones and are the active ingredients in learning to cope with life's setbacks, transforming what starts out as emotional chaos into containable anxiety, so that with each experience you acquire skills that will enable you to cope more effectively next time. Over time, ongoing positive emotions build a lasting personal resource which can be utilised to encourage you to think with more flexibility, openness and creativity, which are important components of good professional practice.

Taking a proactive approach

As discussed in Chapter 6, there are also a number of proactive ways in which you can manage competing demands in the workplace. These include establishing a healthy work/life balance, managing your time effectively, taking breaks from your work, confining your work to your normal hours and place of work wherever possible, and learning to say 'No'. It can also be helpful to recognise your peak energy times, so that you can arrange to do the most demanding tasks when your energy level is at its highest, reserving more routine work for the low points of your daily energy cycle.

Support from others

How would you describe your own experiences of seeking and finding different sources of support from others? What kinds of support are most important to you? See Box 8.2.

Box 8.2 Seeking and finding support

Reflect on your own experiences in your current post:

- What sources of support are available to you?
- Can you identify three resources – people or activities – that you find particularly helpful?
- Can you identify three resources – people or activities – that you find unhelpful?
- Can you identify any gaps?
- What would you add, if anything?

Responses to similar questions among the sample of newly qualified social workers who participated in our study in the south-west are summarised in Table 8.1.

We discuss the central role of supervision for the quality of your practice and professional development in Chapters 4 and 9, so here we will focus on the support provided by colleagues, wider professional networks, and friends and family members.

Table 8.1 Social workers' sources of support

Source of support	Important/very important (%)
Formal, planned supervision	92
Colleagues in same team	92
Other professionals	92
Colleagues elsewhere in same agency	77
Friends and/or family	77
Peer/student from qualifying programme	38
Tutor/teacher from qualifying programme	8

Colleagues

In the early stages, you may well be feeling anxious and in need of reassurance about your practice in a new setting, and it is clear from Table 8.1 that the support of an experienced member of staff in the same team or elsewhere in the organisation can be a valuable resource, not only for emotional support, but also to provide you with opportunities to work alongside them, observing, shadowing or co-working, to build your knowledge and confidence. As discussed in Chapter 3, some organisations have adopted the practice of identifying a particular person to act as a mentor or 'buddy' to support a new member of staff through the first few weeks in post, by offering help, information and advice. The role of buddy is generally short term, and is likely to be most effective and helpful when taken up by a willing volunteer, sited close to you (e.g. in the same team or room).

Mentoring may be a longer-term arrangement, held in place for, say, the first 12 months in a new post. At its best, mentoring should involve a more experienced practitioner guiding and supporting a new member of staff through the initial transition period, smoothing the way by building confidence, knowledge and skills. There are many models of mentoring, and arrangements can vary from an informal personal link to much more formal contract arrangements. There may be some cross-over with a supervisor or line manager, and if you do have a named mentor, it will be important to be clear about respective roles, responsibilities and boundaries. Ideally, a mentor should be outside your line management structure, and there are benefits which parallel what nurses would call 'clinical supervision', including opportunities to:

- discuss your work in confidence with someone who listens and understands the pressures of the job

- get feedback and new ideas about how to deal with work situations

- receive help in dealing with emotions engendered by the work, including stress and exhaustion as well as excitement and happiness

- develop your knowledge of the organisation and how best to use its structures, processes and procedures

- enhance your sense of 'belonging' and value as part of the team.

Wider professional networks

As noted in the introduction to this chapter, there are a number of straightforward or more 'instrumental' reasons for seeking support from a wider network of colleagues, 'specialists' and other professionals. The need, particularly in the early days of a new post (at whatever point in your career), for practical advice, information and assistance will be obvious. As we noted in Chapter 3, time to put together your own list of 'key players', with particular areas of interest or expertise, both inside and outside your own organisation and professional boundaries, should be a key part of the initial orientation into your new surroundings.

Team meetings can also be used to good advantage if time is allowed for sharing common experiences, acknowledging strengths, and providing opportunities to explore problems and possible solutions, rather than simply focusing on bureaucratic allocation and procedural matters. This helps to prevent feelings of isolation in which difficult decisions have to be made alone, without some forum in which to discuss them, either before or after the event.

You might also take the initiative to look for wider support networks through professional associations, websites and associated electronic forums specific to your particular specialism, setting or interest, to establish 'communities of practice' particularly where geographical location is an additional isolating factor. This could be a useful approach to keeping in touch, for instance, with your peer group from university, or establishing a network of contacts following a successful training course.

Friends and family members

Table 8.1 shows that more than three-quarters of the newly qualified social workers who participated in our study placed high importance on the support they received from friends and family members. This informal support, from outside the social work setting, is more valuable perhaps because it is free from the structural and power differentials which are an intrinsic part of organisational life. Friends and family act as a primary resource when moral support, reassurance and understanding are needed, as part of the emotion-focused coping which assists a return to positive, problem-solving strategies. Talking has long been the cornerstone of many psychotherapeutic interventions, helping to ventilate and resolve the thoughts and feelings immediately provoked by stressful situations (Lepore *et al.* 2000), thereby facilitating adjustment to the stressor. William Wordsworth expresses something of the enduring importance of talking in the following line:

> A timely utterance gave that thought relief, and I again am strong.
> (*Intimations of Immortality from Recollections of Early Childhood*)

There are some interesting differences in relation to gender and support (Collins 2008). For instance, it has been shown that the more support a woman receives from her husband or partner, the less conflict she experiences between job and family demands (Berkowitz and Perkins 1984). Women are generally better than men at looking for and providing social support for each other and get more satisfaction from it (Taylor *et al.* 2000). However, although neither so ready to look for nor to provide social support, it has been noted that men frequently receive support from a close female friend or partner (Kirschbaum *et al.* 1995). Taylor *et al.* (2000) have attempted to explain these gender differences as an adaptation by women of the general 'fight or flight' response to threats, transforming this into a 'tend and befriend' approach, incorporating behaviours which focus on nurturing (tending) and gathering into social groups (befriending) in order to reduce risk, threats or stress.

Organisational support

The team

In local authority and joint agency settings, the team is the most-often quoted repository of safety and nurture for newly qualified staff, as demonstrated in Table 8.1, and by the following quotations from the same study.

> **“** Yeah, brilliant, yeah, I will say the one thing that seems to hold social services together is the team, the camaraderie, the support that everybody gets, you do feel part of something. (NQSW)
>
> Yes, I am … I'm well supported and although the rest of the team aren't social work qualified, they're great. (NQSW – Joint Agency Team) **”**

However, social work teams are no longer as straightforward as they used to be. Following the inquiry by Lord Laming (2003) into the death of Victoria Climbié, and the subsequent publication of *Options for Excellence* (Department of Health 2006), the need for coordination between education, health and social care services has been formally recognised in a range of social policies requiring professionals and agencies to work in partnership.

From a professional point of view, the focus on 'working together' starts well before first employment. National occupational standards at qualifying level include a requirement to demonstrate work within multidisciplinary and multi-organisational teams, networks and systems, and this is further reinforced at post-qualifying levels by requirements such as that in England 'to develop and implement effective ways of working in networks across organisational, sectoral and professional boundaries to overcome barriers to multi-agency and multi-disciplinary communication' (GSCC 2006a, p.17).

From a practice point of view, social workers are increasingly finding themselves working in more complex arrangements in which they are part of a number of different networks and teams, comprising members from more than one agency and/or from different professional backgrounds. To confuse the picture further, there are a number of different types of teamworking, which can range from a group of practitioners working together to support a specific child or family, through to a fully integrated service.

The development of broader, multi-agency approaches to working with children and families brings with it a range of advantages, as well as specific challenges. On the positive side, practitioners report high levels of job satisfaction, linked to perceptions of a more creative and holistic approach to delivering services and a 'sense of liberation from bureaucratic or cultural constraints' (Department for Children, Schools and Families (DCSF) 2009). However, there are also a number of challenges which have implications for the availability of support. These include potential conflicts over roles and responsibilities, amidst a range of professional backgrounds and cultures, as well as practitioners undertaking similar tasks but on rather different terms and conditions, as a result of historical agreements applicable to each individual's 'home' agency or profession.

It is possible that you will be joining a number of different groups and teams as a new member during your first 12 months in your new post, and to help you understand something of the functioning of the group, it is worth considering its stage of development in terms of Tuckman's (1965) model, which is summarised in Table 8.2. It is worth bearing in mind that the stages of team formation are not static, and an individual team will move up and down through these different stages at different times as its membership and their circumstances change (see Box 8.3).

Table 8.2 Stages in the formation of a team

Stage	Team behaviour
Forming	Purpose and goals may be unclear Stage marked by formality and politeness
Storming	Tensions emerge; team members struggle for position Leaders have to establish their authority
Norming	Team gains confidence and begins to feel a sense of identity; there is a growing consensus on approaches, goals, communication and leadership; members take on more responsibilities
Performing	Team becomes self-organising; members take full responsibility for tasks and relationships and work proactively for the benefit of the group; team achieves effective and satisfying results and recognises its achievements; levels of trust and confidence are high

Source: adapted from Tuckman (1965)

Box 8.3 Storming or performing?

Apply Tuckman's stages to the groups or teams of which you are a part:

- What stage is each group or team currently at?
- What are the implications for your own support?
- How can you influence the way the groups or teams operate?

Teams can offer you positive support by providing:

- a source of meaning and identity

- learning opportunities, drawing on the interests and expertise of others

- social interactions ranging from satisfactory working relationships through to close friendships

- motivation to keep you going in stressful situations

- shared responsibilities, helping you to build emotional strength and confidence.

On the other hand, teams can have their limitations where:

- team members are negative and unsupportive

- power is abused and decision-making appears driven by politics rather than the needs of service users or team members

- competition between members, for funds or jobs for example, becomes destructive and damaging.

Whatever type of team you are working in when you start a new job, there are some basic characteristics that you will certainly want to know about, which may influence the support that they are likely to offer to a new member. For instance:

- *Stability and state of the team*: If there are several fairly new members of the team, they are likely to remember very well what it was like to be new and welcome you readily. If the team is composed of mainly well-established staff, unaccustomed to change, then it may be more difficult to join in, particularly if there is something of a 'club' culture. This type of team may have become set in its ways and may feel threatened by the changes heralded by a new member. In these circumstances, you may need to tread more carefully.

- *Leadership style*: How hierarchical is the organisational structure? To what extent does the team operate democratically? Are decisions made by consultation or sent down 'from above'?

- *Communication*: How does the team communicate? How often does the whole team come together? What opportunities are there for formal and informal communication?

- *Relationship among members*: Is your team a close-knit community or a loose association of members? How much real collaboration and cooperation is there? What sorts of relationships predominate? See Belbin (2004) for descriptors of different individual roles within teams.

Your answers to some of these questions will help you to form at least an initial understanding of the team's strengths and the way in which it operates. Having gathered this background information you could give some thought to any gaps, and what your own particular contribution to the team could be.

Group support and learning sets

It has been shown (Collins 2008) that, generally speaking, support from colleagues is far more efficacious in buffering the negative effects of workplace stressors than the provision of training in coping skills. The support provided by groups and learning sets has much to recommend it and, linked to the coping strategies discussed in Chapter 7, should help you by:

- encouraging discussion, providing opportunities for 'letting off steam' as an initial coping mechanism in stressful situations

- building consensus and providing you with opportunities to form coalitions and networks which will be important as part of a positive reappraisal approach to coping

- enhancing your own sense of role and mission, to prevent depersonalisation and promote self-detachment to protect against emotional exhaustion

- providing a forum for the wider exploration of the agency's implicit and explicit rules, role ambiguities and possible conflicts, all of which appear in Chapter 7 as primary causes of stress.

It became clear quite early on in our own study that newly qualified social workers, like the one quoted here, needed a safe place in which to discuss their work and find release for their emotional responses to it, which varied from exhaustion and frustration, right through to anger, at times.

> **"** I think there is a level of care and concern but whether it extends beyond 9–5 Monday to Friday I'm not sure. I'm seeing it in front of my eyes. People I thought were very strong are just breaking down in tears ... and I think is anyone actually listening to what's going on? And they're not because they [management] are just driving, this machine just keeps driving and pushing and there's no let up with it ... We're just this sort of cannon fodder if you want, just feeding this machine ... And that's driving my life ... being forced on my life and I'm thinking bloody hell ... We need a revolution to go on here! (NQSW) **"**

In fact, faced with the high levels of stress and anxiety commonly felt in frontline social work practice, it is especially important that you feel that you have 'permission' to express angry feelings appropriately. There is even some evidence to suggest that there is a negative effect on outcomes for service users where anger remains 'cooped up' inside individual workers (Bednar 2003). We have also made reference in Chapter 7 to the negative effects on individual coping where difficulties are internalised and allowed to build up, in the hope that they will disappear. The difficulty for individuals frequently lies in finding a safe forum in which to express emotions appropriately. Supervision or team meetings may very well not provide the right environment for such self-disclosure, especially when you are a new member. In some agencies, groups of workers in a similar situation are facilitated to come together on a regular basis, in addition to their normal supervision, for the purposes of mutual support. Newly qualified social workers are a particularly good example of a readily identifiable group with specific support and development requirements, as the quote from an NQSW illustrates.

> **"** That's been really good, you know. A few of us get together and talk about where we are and how practice relates to university, or how it doesn't quite often. (NQSW) **"**

A peer support group or learning set can provide the time and opportunity needed to consider yourself and your own needs in an appropriate environment. Ideally, such meetings should be held away from individual workplaces, and preferably be facilitated by someone external to the agency's line management structures. Arrangements should also be fixed in advance, and at regular intervals, so that you can block out the time in your diary and firmly commit to being part of the group. There is a responsibility on the part of each member to attend regularly and to make an active contribution to the group for mutual benefit. Learning set meetings then provide members with a safe space in which to express their feelings, giving access to the social support of others in a similar position, as well as offering a forum for the exchange of information and advice. Join if your agency already has these groups in place, and where the message has not yet taken root, seize the initiative and suggest some of the benefits to your training or staff development department.

Training and development activities

Nearly all newly qualified social workers are enthusiastic about taking on new tasks, developing new areas and continuing to learn. One way in which organisations can create a satisfying climate for social workers is by offering frequent opportunities for them to attend conferences, seminars, workshops and training programmes, and local authorities and larger voluntary sector organisations will definitely have a range of courses on offer. Much of the early in-house training offered to you as an NQSW is likely to be practical information or task based, focusing on induction requirements and preparation for taking on more complex work. As well as focusing on enhancing the skills needed to undertake work with service users, you might also try to seek out and prioritise some sessions covering the following areas to support your own development, recognising the additional stresses of transitional change from qualification into the workplace:

- stress management and resilience

- coping skills

- managing emotions

- time management

- managing change.

As the quotations from two NQSWs illustrate, it is not unusual for there to be little structuring of in-house training and continuing professional development opportunities, so you may need a good deal of determination, initiative and individual motivation to seek out what is available and how to book yourself a place.

> **"** I'm not sure really. I don't think they have an actual policy about how it works. It's just that some people seem to do post-qualifying training and others ...never do it. (NQSW)
>
> Overall, there's a good level of training offered ... but it's a bit hit and miss who gets on it and who doesn't ... and it's, well you pick up the phone and find out what's on and you go and hassle your manager to give you a signature. (NQSW) **"**

Organisations employing NQSWs have a responsibility to provide you with professional development opportunities, but it is your responsibility to ensure that you make the best of what is available to you, in order to:

- meet your changing needs as you progress through induction and transition

- expand your own areas of special interest, considering how these 'fit' with the organisation's overall aims and vision

- explore opportunities to broaden your experiences in a range of settings and contexts.

It is also important to remember to record what you have done: for post-registration training and learning (PRTL) purposes, to update your personal development plan (PDP), and to take the PDP into supervision and appraisal so that each individual activity is brought together to provide a whole picture of your ongoing development. There is more on using personal development planning in Chapter 12.

Key considerations in finding support

- The support you need cannot be found in one place. Access to a range of different sources and types of support, to meet your needs in different situations and at different times, is an essential requirement for all social workers, and time spent in developing a robust system for yourself is a sound investment for your future well-being.

- Although it may feel imperative to prioritise tasks focused on service user needs, there is an equal imperative to take time to find a safe place in which you can explore the impact of the work, and in which you have permission to express your feelings. If there are specific groups for newly qualified social workers, you should make regular attendance a personal commitment.

- The team is an important source of support, but it is not a static entity, and its character will change and evolve over time as well as in response to new pressures and personalities.

Chapter 9

Taking Part in Supervision

- The purpose and functions of supervision
- The dynamic structure of supervision
- Making the most of supervision
- Managing the tensions in supervision
- Key considerations for making the most of supervision

Supervision is widely recognised as a key learning and support mechanism, not only in the early stages but also throughout the whole of your professional career in social work, and this chapter is therefore dedicated entirely to the subject of supervision. The chapter is called 'Taking Part in Supervision' to emphasise the two-way nature of the process, and the need for each participant to take responsibility for their part in establishing a supportive 'supervisory alliance'. The following comments by NQSWs are typical of those made by many social workers, newly qualified or not, working in children and families settings, when asked about their experiences of supervision.

> **"** What we do is we review the cases very quickly ... to see, as much as anything else, if there's any more space to fit some more cases in and it's a question of 'have you done this on time, have you done that on time' because my manager is under pressure [from senior managers].
>
> I'd like more time, more direction in terms of you know being able to sit down and get guidance when I'm approaching tasks.

> If the managers aren't given more time or there are no more managers, then what gives? Well it's the time particularly to reflect on cases … what did you do … what worked … what didn't … what have you learned …That's missing from all of our supervision.
>
> (Social workers – 12 months post-qualification) **"**

As these comments reflect significant dissatisfaction with supervision arrangements, it might be helpful to review your own experiences, using the exercise in Box 9.1.

Box 9.1 Supervision style

Thinking about your experiences of supervision, either in your present job or from your qualifying training, what did you learn about:

- What supervision means for you?
- How you want to use supervision?
- What worries you most about supervision?
- What sort of supervision seems to suit you best?

The exercise may have pointed out a number of tensions inherent in the supervisory relationship, which may be particularly acutely felt when you are new to the organisation. So what should supervision do?

The purpose and functions of supervision

The overall purpose of supervision is to improve the services that are offered to service users and carers. Benefits for service users and carers may accrue directly, as supervision helps you to think about the best ways of helping on an individual basis, as well as indirectly, as better services are known to be delivered by satisfied social workers who feel that they are valued members of a committed team.

According to Kadushin (1976, p.229) supportive supervision should 'allay anxiety, reduce guilt, increase certainty and conviction, relieve dissatisfaction, fortify flagging faith, affirm and reinforce the worker's assets, replenish depleted self-esteem, nourish and enhance the capacity for adaptation, alleviate psychological pain, restore emotional equilibrium, comfort, bolster and refresh'. Such an extensive list makes it clear why supervision is one of the most important mechanisms available to organisations to support and develop their staff. Definitions of supervision in social work have been evolving since the 1930s (Morrison 2001; Robinson 1936; Shulman 1982). According to Middleman and Rhodes (1980), for example, the supervisor–worker relationship is the key encounter where the influence of organisational authority and professional identity meet. Although there are some significant differences between the various definitions of supervision, there is broad agreement about the three main functions, which are as follows.

1. *Normative*: sometimes called organisational or managerial

   - implementing and monitoring policies, procedures, planning and budgeting

   - monitoring and auditing casework

   - ensuring competent, accountable practice.

2. *Formative*: sometimes called educational or developmental

   - developing professional skills, techniques and boundaries

   - developing knowledge, drawing on detailed discussions of individual work.

3. *Restorative*: sometimes called personal or supportive

   - providing emotional support and team building

   - promoting communication, coordination and cooperation.

The dynamic structure of supervision

It was Mattinson (1981) who first argued that there are not two but three participants in a supervision session – supervisor, supervisee and service user – each of whom exerts an influence over the discussions which take place. In order to understand how the multitude of

Figure 9.1 The participants in supervision

functions and tasks of supervision are interrelated and can be successfully managed, Hughes and Pengelly (1997) developed a model based around the connections between two triangles, the first of which (in Figure 9.1) illustrates the presence of the three participants.

- *The supervisor*, often (although not always) representing line-management authority and agency accountability.

- *The practitioner*, bringing the results of direct work and evidence-gathering with service users, professionals and other care workers.

- *The service user*, with needs, capacities, demands and rights.

In addition to the three participants, the three key functions of supervision – normative, formative and restorative – can also be represented at each corner of a triangle, as illustrated in Figure 9.2.

Figure 9.2 The key functions of supervision

There is a dynamic tension, within and between the corners of the two triangles, as the key relationships and issues involved in any situation present themselves. Although the corners of the two triangles never completely overlap, there are specific connections between the three *functions* of supervision and its three *participants*. To take full account of the complexity of managing all six corners, supervision needs to be 'a flexible space', and the triangle model is particularly helpful if you think of the sides as 'elastic' boundaries, within which the participants can migrate from one corner to another, and functions can be prioritised in different combinations, as discussions about the work develop and progress. These competing tensions will cause the shape of the triangles to change as the priorities ebb and flow. For instance, in the participants' triangle, it may be necessary for both supervisor and practitioner to focus entirely on a service user's rights, at which point all three participants migrate into the service user's corner for a time. Similarly, in the functions triangle, developing a new area of knowledge may emerge as a specific priority, so that the focus will be entirely on the 'educational' corner, with little or no attention being paid to the organisational or personal corners for a limited period.

As Hughes and Pengelly (1997) suggest, visualising the processes of supervision in this way, applying the two triangles across the competing tensions of your own work, should help you to:

- keep all three participants and all three functions of supervision in mind, even if the focus on each element is different at any one time

- understand the dynamic interrelationship between the participants and the functions of supervision, and deal with them in a more integrated way

- ensure that no corner is ignored or avoided for any length of time.

Making the most of supervision

The work you do and how you do it is at the heart of any type of supervision, and to make the most of what supervision has to offer, you need to ensure that you take a proactive stance in negotiating what you want and need from supervision. The initial arrangements that you will need to make for supervision were considered as part of the induction processes explored in Chapter 4, including the advantages of developing a written agreement.

Expectations, hopes and fears

In a study by Carroll and Gilbert (2005, p.11) a group of supervisees used the following metaphors to describe what supervision meant to them:

- a torch – which illuminates my practice

- a container – where I feel safe and held

- a mirror – where I see myself and my work

- a playpen – where we play with ideas, feelings, intuitions, theories

- a dance – where we learn how to work together in harmony

- a classroom – which contains two learners

- a thermometer – to gauge intellectual, emotional, psychological and social climates

- a sculpture – where I am being fashioned into something yet to be.

You might like to think about what supervision means to you, and begin your first supervision with your new supervisor by exploring your hopes and fears, and sharing your expectations of a good working alliance. Completing the statements in Box 9.2 about the process separately from your supervisor, and then comparing responses, could form part of a helpful warm-up exercise.

Whatever your hopes and fears, you are not an 'empty vessel' waiting to be filled, or working to become a 'clone' of your supervisor. You will develop your own style and approaches to practice. In Chapter 1, we characterised the development of professional expertise as requiring rather more than an apprenticeship approach, and so it is with supervision which should enable you to forge your own identity within the overall boundaries of the profession (Carroll and Gilbert

2005). Given that the focus is on your practice and professional development, it is incumbent on you to take whatever action is needed to get what you want and need from supervision. Channelling your initial enthusiasm appropriately is probably a good place to start. You need to ensure that supervision includes proper development planning, linked to your previous work history, training and placement experiences, and that, in consultation with your supervisor, you use all of this information to set realistic and achievable goals, both in the short term and longer term, that will foster a sense of growth and accomplishment for you. If your initial enthusiasm is not harnessed appropriately, there is a danger that you could be thrown headlong into work in quite an unprotected way, or inadvertently expose yourself to hurt and rejection from service users, leaving you feeling that you are in the wrong job. In order to avoid these sorts of problems, Brown and Bourne (1996) recommend that early supervision sessions should incorporate a 'stress check'.

Box 9.2 Supervision: expectations, hopes and fears

Complete the following statements in relation to your new supervision arrangements, and ask your supervisor to do the same:

- I am expecting supervision to be …
- I am expecting supervision to provide …
- What I fear most in supervision is …
- What I value most in supervision is …
- I hope that supervision will be …
- What interests me about supervision is …

How similar are your responses to those of your supervisor?

What differences are there, and are there any actions you could take, either together or separately, to reduce their impact?

Stress check

We have earlier argued that a certain amount of stress can be good for you, encouraging you to work at your best without allowing the strains of the job to become overwhelming. The stress check suggested by Brown and Bourne (1996), which is illustrated in Figure 9.3, involves mapping the potential and actual stressors that exist within four interconnected systems: your personal life, your practice, your team and the wider agency.

Figure 9.3 Mapping potential stressors

The four interconnected systems and examples of their potential stressors are as follows:

- *your personal life*: relationship difficulties; illness; financial difficulties; bereavement

- *your practice*: violence; abuse; service users' disclosures; large workload

- *your team*: personal conflicts; bullying; isolation; colleagues' stresses

- *the wider agency*: new procedures; competition for promotion; reorganisation.

Each stressor can be considered in relation to its impact on you and how you are managing it, and through regular recording and review, any trends that might otherwise not be apparent can be identified. Using the familiar ecological model to address what might be a sensitive area in this way, early on in supervision, should establish stress management as a central aspect of the routine of supervision discussions, rather than something which is either minimised or ignored all together.

Supervision style

The style in which supervision is both given and received will also be important aspects of the relationship. Heron (1975) divided any process of facilitation or enabling, of which supervision would certainly be one, into six categories as follows:

- *prescriptive*: giving advice; being directive

- *informative*: being didactic; giving instruction and information

- *confrontative*: challenging; giving direct feedback

- *cathartic*: releasing tension

- *catalytic*: being reflective, encouraging self-directed problem-solving

- *supportive*: offering approval, confirmation and validation.

The priority given to each of these categories, and the balance between them, might usefully be the subject of some discussion with your supervisor as you set up your supervision agreement. An exploration of your preferences, and the importance that each of you places on any specific activity, might be helpful in trying to understand and meld together both sides of a healthy 'alliance'.

It is not uncommon to arrive for supervision stressed, anxious, angry or afraid. These feelings are all part of your perceptions of and responses to your experiences of work with service users, and with other members of the team or the wider organisation. In fact, you might consider that your usual equilibrium and the way in which you normally respond to challenges have been disturbed. This very disturbance to your normal way of being can either generate new energy, which can provide the opportunity for developing more successful ways of dealing with your experiences, or engender feelings of inadequacy and hopelessness, as a precursor to some more defensive or destructive action. Any of the following expressions could indicate that your very 'being' has been challenged (Brown and Bourne 1996, p.119) in a way with which it has been difficult to come to terms:

'Why me?'

'I can't understand it, I thought we had such a good relationship.'

'I never believed people could be like that.'

'I don't know who I am any longer.'

'I can't believe this has happened.'

'It feels as though the rug has been pulled from under me.'

'I've completely lost it, nothing seems straightforward any more.'

Although perhaps triggered by a particular event, these feelings are more likely to be part of an ongoing process of encountering and attempting to resolve 'crisis situations' which transcend your prior personal and practice experiences. Using crisis intervention theory to shine a light on your own situation might offer you some useful insights into what, in these circumstances, will be most helpful to you in a supervision session. Roberts' (2000) seven stage model of crisis intervention, set out in Table 9.1, recommends a process which is equally applicable to a resolution of your own feelings, including finding support, restoring your confidence and building future resilience.

Table 9.1 Seven stage model of crisis intervention

1. Immediate response
2. Establish rapport
3. Define the major problem
4. Explore feelings
5. Consider alternative responses
6. Make an action plan
7. Review and follow-up support

Source: adaoted from Roberts (2000)

The model suggests that when equilibrium is disturbed and usual coping strategies have failed, you need an immediate response. This is where you may need to make use of a manager's 'open door' policy or other informal arrangements to begin with. Let us hope that the rapport that you already have with your supervisor will provide the reassurance you need that help is available. You should enter supervision prepared to be open and honest about all of the significant elements of your current situation, and exactly what has brought you to this 'crisis' point. Supervision should provide the safe, understanding and empathic environment in which to express your feelings, but if another setting would be better for you (e.g. a peer support group) then this should be discussed in supervision. Considering alternative responses will involve taking a look, with your supervisor, at your coping strategies and social networks, with a view to suggesting different ways in which you can respond, or different resources on which you can call for support. Any meeting with your supervisor should end with a summary of outcomes, which might include one or two clear goals in relation to your coping strategies.

Meeting arrangements

Over three-quarters of the social workers in our own study identified supervision as one of the most important sources of support, guidance and advice during their first year in employment, but nearly all of them (85%) also reported that insufficient time was allocated to it.

It is not always easy to prioritise supervision in a busy workplace, yet if it is to be given significance and assume its proper importance, arrangements that have been agreed should not be surrendered lightly, on either side. The knowledge that you can rely on it to be there, without question, is one of the most important understandings that may not actually appear in writing in your supervision agreement. In the early stages you are likely to use supervision as something of a refuge, giving you time to stand back, take stock, and restore your equilibrium. If there is any doubt about its availability – that it can be easily brushed aside in favour of competing priorities – then your confidence and self-assurance might easily be undermined or damaged. The firm commitment to regular sessions will help to develop a deeper sense of direction and purpose for supervision as a process of relationship-building, rather than a succession of unconnected encounters for administrative purposes. It is also worth giving some thought to where you will meet, so that it can be somewhere open to least interruptions which can detract from the flow of thoughts and ideas, particularly if you have waited for the right time to broach a more sensitive or difficult subject.

Having agreed on frequency, duration and venue as part of your supervision agreement, it is a good idea to book a programme of meeting dates, possibly for the year, in both diaries, to confirm your joint commitment to the arrangements. It is inevitable that, from time to time, other commitments may need to take precedence over supervision, but when any particular session is disrupted in this way there will be an immediate reminder that a meeting was due and an alternative date needs to be agreed without delay.

Boundaries

You will already know that all kinds of personal background information can affect your practice as a social worker, and although this does not necessarily entitle your supervisor to any information about your personal life, some disclosure is likely to make the relationship more effective. Almost any social work situation has the potential to produce or reproduce personal feelings which need to be shared and explored in order to enable you to practise effectively and maintain your well-being. However, it can feel risky in the early stages of your supervision relationship to disclose personal information or feelings. Boundaries around the supervisory relationship, what is professional and what is personal, should help to clarify matters and create a safe and trusting environment for open discussion. In general, personal material will be relevant only where it is directly affecting the work you are doing, or vice versa. If an initial exploration of personal issues reveals that there are deeper matters that cannot be met within the bounds of a routine supervision session, then a good supervisor might suggest that they are either addressed in a separate meeting, or perhaps through personal counselling. The latter option may be something which is available within your employing agency, or may require self-referral to another agency. The key message here is that, even if they cannot be resolved in supervision, the importance of these personal feelings should not be ignored or denied.

How you manage the boundaries around confidentiality will also be an important part of the supervision agreement, and the need to be completely clear on the detail of what can and cannot be shared is particularly relevant where your supervisor is also your line manager. It is not a good idea to make a tacit assumption that everything said will be treated in confidence, only to find at a later date that confidentiality has been breached. It is therefore better to try to specify in advance what sort of information would need to be taken outside the boundaries of the supervision relationship, together with when, how and to whom it would be taken. Although it will not be possible to cover every eventuality, by being as specific as possible you minimise the risk of misunderstandings and the possibility of feeling let down or betrayed.

Preparation

Preparation is important, not least because it allows you to take control of the agenda and to ensure that you get what you want from supervision. You can make sure that you address the issues you wish to deal with and whatever is important to you. Preparation also provides the opportunity to sort out your thoughts, and clarify your thinking about all kinds of work events, not limited only to those which you want to discuss in your next supervision session. Without this more structured approach to your thinking, work can seem like a relentless stream of events, each of which requires your attention before you are confronted by the next event, and so on. It is not always the most obviously important events that are the most productive to deal with in supervision. Sometimes, thinking more broadly around apparently trivial incidents can reveal important insights that would benefit from further discussion. When you are thinking about your practice, there is also a natural tendency to focus on the things that have gone wrong. Yet, it is important that you also remember to reflect on situations that went well, where you feel that you did a piece of really good work, because trying to analyse those situations might also help you to understand better how you can replicate them.

Asking yourself a few questions about your work can be a great help in getting the best out of each supervision session: see Box 9.3.

Box 9.3 Supervision: preparation questionnaire

As part of your preparation routine for each supervision session, take a few moments to answer the following questions to inform your agenda:

- Which situations do you feel you dealt with well?

- Which situations did not go so well?

- Were there any situations in which you didn't know what to do?

- Is there any service user relationship or situation which is causing you particular concern?

- Is there any staff relationship – in your own team or other professional or agency – which is causing you particular concern?

Source: adapted from Royal College of Nursing (RCN 1999)

If you are keeping a reflexive journal, this can be of enormous help in the preparation process. By looking through your journal, you can see whether there are any particular issues or incidents that stand out that you would like to discuss in supervision. You might also identify trends or repeating patterns in your thinking, doing or feeling that might otherwise not have been apparent and which it could be important to explore in more detail, with the benefit of your supervisor's perspective.

Your personal development plan (PDP) should also be a useful source of prompts for supervision, helping you to make the links between your current and future workload – the areas of strength currently being evidenced and the areas for future development, for instance as part of a specific piece of allocated work, or by taking up a shadowing or co-working opportunity, or through specific training. Articulating learning objectives for yourself, as well as in consultation with your supervisor, allows you to develop clear goals towards which you are working, and which your supervisor can monitor for you to provide ongoing feedback on your progress. If it makes a regular appearance in supervision sessions, your PDP will ensure that professional development has at least some place on the agenda.

Talking and listening

Talking and listening are probably the key interpersonal skills that are the foundation of your social work practice, and they are no less central to developing a trusting, open and honest relationship within supervision. To get the best out of supervision you need to pay attention both to what you say and to what is said to you.

First, when you set out to describe a situation, try to be as concise as possible, keeping to the point and providing only the details that are necessary to provide an appropriate overview for your supervisor. This will maximise the time available to you to go through the important issues thoroughly. Guard against any tendency to occupy the time in supervision with every single detail of a case as a defence or avoidance mechanism, preventing the central difficulties and dilemmas being brought out into the open for discussion.

As already noted, you should try to contribute positive as well as negative material to supervision. There can be as much benefit to your learning from analysing a situation that went well as from discussing something that did not.

A good supervisor will want to 'establish an atmosphere of competence' (Morrison 2001) by eliciting from you some of the pieces of work that have gone well and produced positive outcomes, however small those may have been, before you discuss any problems. Without this sort of structure, there is a real danger that supervision can become overburdened with problems, focusing exclusively on risks, weaknesses, failings and limitations, thereby undermining your confidence and tending to magnify feelings of confusion or inadequacy which are common for any new recruit.

Supervision is of course a dialogue, a two-way process, within which, quite often, it is surprisingly easy for people to misunderstand each other. Reflecting back what has been said to you is a skill that you will regularly use with service users, and this same skill can be equally helpful in making sure that you have understood (and not distorted) what has been said in supervision. Paraphrasing or making a short summary, reflected back to your supervisor, will allow you to correct any misunderstandings and clarify decisions and plans for action which can then be accurately recorded.

Feedback and criticism

An important part of the dialogue in supervision will be giving and receiving feedback. Again, the general 'rules' for giving feedback will be familiar to you from your direct work, but here too it might be helpful to consider these in relation to your supervision. Good feedback should be clear, owned, regular, balanced and specific. If it is not, you can ask for clarification – you do not have to be a passive recipient in the feedback process. Try to receive others' feedback as *their* experiences of you, in which it is often sufficient to hear and simply acknowledge what has been said. It is quite common in the early stages of a career to feel that any difficulties are the equivalent of personal failings which reflect directly on your competence and suitability, rather than challenges which, in time, you will successfully overcome. Difficulties can arise if you react immediately to perceived criticism, without taking the time to listen properly to what was actually being said. Careful listening is required even in uncomfortable circumstances, in which you take time to think the situation through. Try not to automatically agree or disagree, or compulsively to explain. The skill here is in recognising when to be assertive and when it is more appropriate to take time to reflect on what you have heard. Everybody makes mistakes or fails to meet the standard that they would ideally like to meet from time to time. Judging yourself too harshly can mean that you shut down and block out what happened, rather than being open to discussion and learning from it. Occasionally, you may find that something that you felt was reasonable at the time later evokes strong emotions. Delayed reactions of this sort are not uncommon, and you may find it helpful to discuss these feelings and their causes with your supervisor at your next meeting. If you do not raise them, your supervisor will have no way of knowing how you felt, and keeping them to yourself can easily build up resentment which will doubtless emerge to cause problems later. Of course, all of this requires a measure of courage on your part, as well as trust in your supervisor. Usually, trust comes with knowing your supervisor well, which takes time, but building a more trusting relationship will enable you to start letting go of defensive feelings and to begin to discuss important issues more freely, without feeling that you are being judged.

Blocks

The learning function of supervision draws heavily on the reflection–action model which may be familiar to you from the four stages of Kolb's (1984) experiential learning cycle, set out in Figure 9.4.

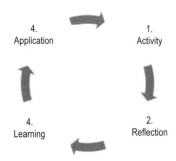

Figure 9.4 Four stages of the experiential learning cycle (adapted from Kolb 1984)

While you would normally expect to be moving smoothly through each stage of the cycle as you develop your professional practice, it is quite possible that, at times, you may find yourself 'stuck' at a particular stage. For example, you may become so stressed with a heavy workload that you are unable to do your work in the way you would like to meet the standards that you expect from yourself, so that you are stuck in Stage 1, or you may be so worried about 'getting it right' and proving yourself in a new job that you shut down reflection by excluding any reference to areas that are not going well, becoming stuck in Stage 2. Alternatively, you may feel that it is 'too risky' to admit to not knowing something and avoid asking for the help that you need, so that learning fails to occur (Stage 3), or you may be tempted to take on too much, too quickly, and in a whirlwind of frenetic activity allow yourself no time to consider changes and apply what you have learned (Stage 4). It is possible to become stuck in the learning cycle at any stage in your professional development, and if you recognise any of these blocks to progression, you should consider taking your thoughts and feelings into supervision. Framing the difficulty in terms of a block in the learning cycle may make it easier for you to initiate discussion in order to find the help that will, in Kadushin's words, 'comfort, bolster and refresh your certainty and conviction' (Kadushin 1976, p.229)

Recording

Your supervision agreement should include a section about how the sessions are to be recorded. The written record will allow you to review what happened, and provide you with a summary of what action was agreed. A useful format for supervision notes (Carroll and Gilbert 2005) might include the headings set out in Table 9.2.

Table 9.2 Supervision notes: format

Issues raised in this session	
Client issues	Intervention issues
Supervisee issues	Supervisor issues
Organisational issues	Learning objectives/training issues
Action points	
Signatures	

When you come to prepare for the next session, notes of the previous session will be helpful to keep track of the key action points and how your practice has developed. You can use your supervision notes to pick up any key concepts, and indicate how, when and where you have applied them. Used in this way they become integrated into your day-to-day practice, and might also make a useful adjunct to your reflexive journal, allowing you to take a proactive role in summarising your learning in a more global way.

Limits

It has been shown (Rauktis and Koeske 1994) that supportive supervision has a consistently positive effect on job satisfaction, bolstering the psychological and interpersonal resources that enable you to cope and deliver effective job performance for the benefit of service users. This process is represented diagrammatically in Figure 9.5.

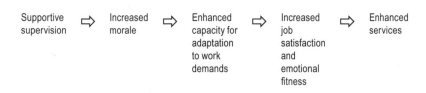

Figure 9.5 Impact of supportive supervision on job satisfaction

There is, however, one important limiting factor to bear in mind. When work demands are high, emotionally supportive supervision loses some of its benefits. Even highly supportive supervision cannot overcome a work environment in which demands have become excessive. You, your supervisor and your agency must be aware of these constraints, recognising the point when altering work demand is the only appropriate response to ensure that you can maintain your well-being, morale and effectiveness. If this point is not recognised by others, you might need to take the lead in supervision discussions, suggesting appropriate amendments, as the newly qualified social worker quoted here did.

> ❝ I went to my boss and said 'Look, I can't cope with this any more. You've got to tell me how to sort this out'. ... so we broke it down and said this is what we need to do. So it became a very practical task and that helped. (NQSW) ❞

Other suggestions that you could take to supervision when workload demands are outstripping your capacity to cope might include some of the following:

- sorting out priorities for individual cases or tasks

- agreeing a temporary reduction in your overall caseload

- reviewing and adjusting previously agreed deadlines or timetables

- sharing responsibility (e.g. with a co-worker or supervisor) for complex pieces of work/decisions

- achieving a better balance of work (e.g. including some less problematic cases)

- weaving some training into your diary.

Managing the tensions in supervision

Previous experiences

Previous experiences of supervision can have a strong influence on your current attitudes and how well you feel the purposes of supervision are met. A bad experience can make you wary of entering into another potentially unsatisfactory situation. On the other hand, a really good experience can make you apprehensive that any new arrangements will not match up to the standard that you have come to expect and rely on.

Receiving support

Receiving support is an area to which social workers can sometimes apply double standards, preferring the relative safety of the provider role. While people who use services are encouraged to identify their needs (as well as their strengths), there is a tendency, widely rein-forced in the culture of some workplaces, to deny your own needs on the grounds that you should be able to cope and that to have needs implies weakness or dependency. The importance of guarding against the tendency to use supervision as a process only for dealing with problems was considered in Chapter 4, but is significant enough to bear reiteration here too.

Defensive routines

Personal inhibition and defensive reactions can be major impediments to the establishment of a supportive 'supervisory alliance'. Have you ever found yourself saying, thinking or feeling some of the following defensive routines (Hawkins and Shohet 2006)?

> 'Yes, yes, I've already thought of that.'

> 'I'll just keep talking, and give you every single detail.'

> 'It's all "done and dusted" – no problems. All finished.'

> 'I know I've made a mess with this one.'

> 'I know you're not going to be very happy with this but…'

The focused, one-to-one attention in supervision can often feel like scrutiny, in which you are very much on the spot. This has been memorably expressed by one newly qualified social worker with whom we spoke as 'snoopervision'.

> ❝ It's an interesting one because the pressures that are being put on managers are such that supervision is changing from supervision to 'snoopervision' to coin a phrase, and our managers are now required to do two file audits every supervision to check that you've got all the documents in there, and that they are up to date and in the right sections. (NQSW) ❞

Conflict of roles

The need for supervision to involve an element of 'snoopervision' is evident in the key messages from an analysis of child care inspection findings (Pont 2000) which looked at various aspects of the tasks of assessment, including supervision. The key failings found by inspectors, summarised by Gordon and Hendry (2001, p.153), are very clear:

- infrequent and unstructured supervision, with interruptions

- inadequate recording of supervision

- lack of expertise and specialist knowledge of supervisors

- lack of rigour in ensuring compliance with policies and procedures

- failure to challenge decisions and lack of rigour in examining the basis for decisions

- failure to record decisions on case files or routinely to monitor case files

- failure to address the professional development needs of workers.

With managers required to look for administrative compliance at the same time as social workers are seeking support and guidance, there is an inherent mismatch of expectations from a single supervisory process. And, as the comments from supervisors illustrate, managers are often doing their job with very little specific training or preparation for their role.

❝ It sounds a bit negative but yes, that was my experience ... [when I was promoted] ... you get a new office and you just get on with it.

The training courses that are set up often don't meet the need because they're too late and they're not directed at what you're doing.

I don't think there is a very good programme really for managers – one minute you're a social worker and the next minute you're a manager and you're just expected to get on with it and you apply, well it's a bit how you learn to be a parent really, you come through by osmosis and you've been working for a manager and you probably try and apply what you consider to be the best from what you've experienced.

(First line managers in statutory agencies) **❞**

Evaluation

We began the chapter by emphasising the centrality of learning to the supervision process and the two-way nature of a successful alliance between supervisee and supervisor. Taking this to its logical conclusion, and bringing both aspects together, 'learning from the learning' will be maximised where there are regular and structured opportunities for honest and open reflection built into the processes, to complete a feedback cycle for both parties to the supervision agreement.

As you settle into your supervision arrangements, you and your supervisor might like to evaluate how well a particular supervision session has gone by answering the following questions:

- What went particularly well or badly in this session?

- Were we communicating effectively with each other?

- What did we not talk about, and why?

- What, if any, external factors affected the session?

- What three actions could improve the quality of future sessions?

(Adapted from Carroll and Gilbert 2005)

An alternative approach would be to complete the questionnaire below (which is phrased as though from your supervisor, in order to provide an opportunity for feedback from you as supervisee) at some time during your first year in post.

- Am I providing the sort of supervision you need?

- Is the supervision relationship productive? Anything we need to discuss?

- Is the feedback I give clear, regular, balanced and specific enough?

- Is there a good balance of support and challenge in our supervision?

- Are there areas that we do not talk about that should be the focus of a conversation?

- Do our discussions make an impact on your practice?

- What seems to you to be the next challenge in your development?

- What is most helpful about our supervision arrangement? What least helpful?

- Is there anything that you would like me to stop doing? Start doing? Increase? Decrease?

- Are we being accountable in our supervision? To service users? To the organisation? To the profession?

(Adapted from Carroll and Gilbert 2005)

Key considerations for making the most of supervision

- There are three 'participants' in supervision (the supervisor, the practitioner and the service user) and three broad functions (organisational, educational, personal), all of which need to be kept in mind.

- Supervision is identified as one of the most important sources of support and guidance by most newly qualified social workers, but the majority also report that insufficient time is allocated to it, so ensure that you and your supervisor give it the priority that it deserves.

- Supervision is likely to be most effective when you play an active part in setting the agenda and prepare properly for each session. The more you put into your supervision, the more you are likely to get out of it.

- Remember that supervision, on its own, also has its limits – if the work demands being placed on you are simply too great you need to do something to change your workload, rather than just talking about the effect it is having on you and your service users.

Part IV

Going the Distance

As your day-to-day practice becomes more streamlined and you deal more confidently with the range of tasks allocated to you, Part IV considers the influence of the organisation on you and conversely how you can begin to have some influence on the organisation. 'Going the Distance' also explores some of the frameworks for progression, promotion and what will be needed to continue your professional development for the future.

Part IV aims to help you to develop a better understanding of how your own position, practice and role 'fits' within the overall organisation, taking account of three primary aspects – structure, culture and climate – which will have the greatest impact on your experience of the organisation and the quality of your working life. Chapter 10 'Working in a Satisfying Climate' returns to look again at the team and teamwork as we consider your development as an 'effective operator' within your organisational context.

Chapter 11 'Managing Increasing Complexity' explores some of the links between critical reflection, reflective practice, learning organisations and organisations that learn. Some of these ideas take us back to the discussions of development of professional expertise in Chapter 1 as you move on in your practice, absorbing new and more challenging experiences and working with greater complexity and increasing uncertainty.

Chapter 12 'Moving Forward: Continuing Professional Development' discusses the dual concepts of lifelong learning and continuing professional development and how these ideas have been applied more specifically to social work through the recently established registration and re-registration requirements of the regulatory councils in each UK country as well as the different approaches adopted to the first year in practice for newly qualified staff and the wider post-qualifying frameworks for education and training in social work.

Chapter 10

Working in a
Satisfying Climate

- Understanding the organisation
- Becoming an effective organisational operator
- Key considerations for working in a satisfying climate

Much of this chapter is concerned with strategies, structures and cultures over which you may feel, particularly as a new member of staff, you have little power and influence. However, developing a better understanding of how your own position, practice and role 'fits' within an overall corporate plan should help to enhance your ability to become an effective professional. By maintaining an active stance, in which you recognise and take responsibility for your own role, you are also likely to become a more satisfied member of the team.

Understanding the organisation

There are three primary aspects of the organisation which will have an impact on how you experience your place within it and the quality of your working life. Broadly, these are its structure and strategies, culture and climate. None of these elements is static, and each has a dynamic interrelation with the others, in constant flux as different imperatives, political and personal, financial and strategic, wax and wane. You might think of this 'organisational triangle' as similar to the Bermuda triangle in which people, rather than ships, can disappear unless certain precautions are taken.

Structure and strategy

We have already referred in Chapter 4 to the importance of obtaining an organisational structure diagram as part of your induction programme, to help you visualise your place within the corporate picture. Without a clear understanding about the roles and responsibilities of different staff within the organisation, confused or conflicting messages can arise which exacerbate feelings of division between frontline workers and their line managers, and a 'them and us' culture can take root.

The physical environment also plays an important part in shaping your relationship with work. For example, where the office building itself is situated in the community, how accessible it is and what security measures are in place may be important factors affecting your day-to-day comings and goings. Inside, the increasing trend towards open plan office accommodation has advantages in that the closeness of team members can be supportive, but there can also be disadvantages, if there is limited privacy and you feel that you are under constant scrutiny.

At the head of the most common hierarchical, bureaucratic agency structure, strategic managers have been called the 'social architects' of the organisation, responsible for designing its purposes, vision and values. The vision – where we are going – and the strategies – how we will get there – will be passed down to be enacted by those in the tiers below. Not infrequently, there is a significant gap between what strategic managers say in a mission statement and what is actually carried out in the organisation, and we certainly found examples of this in our study.

> **"** At the corporate induction the director was saying you must keep the learning going and sign up for PQ without delay and then my manager at the time was saying, no, I haven't got the time for that. I'm not going to support you. I'm not going to give you the time off. (NQSW) **"**

First line managers occupy a pivotal position in a hierarchical structure because they have key responsibilities in two directions, which can sometimes operate in opposition to one another.

❝ I suppose the most difficult thing is managing time and managing competing demands from below and above really. You are very much in the middle of the sandwich I think as a first line manager. (Line manager) **❞**

They are charged with implementing the policies and strategies handed down to them from the higher tiers, and for directing the day-to-day work, while also fostering positive attitudes and beliefs in the organisational mission among frontline staff who they supervise and support in the delivery of services. The ways in which your manager is able to deal with these tensions will certainly influence your opinion of their 'organisational effectiveness'. There is more on leadership and being led in Chapter 11.

Often promoted from a professional practice background, first line managers frequently find that they lack some of the leadership and management skills, related to the specific task of managing a social work child care team, as first line managers from our study attested.

❝ I think it was after about 9 months that I was sent on some training – about supervision – so that was nice – you do it first and then get taught how to do it. I don't think there's a very good programme really for managers.

The training courses that are set up often don't meet the need because they're too late and they're not directed specifically at what you're doing.

(First line managers in local authority teams) **❞**

Although not specifically concerned with social care, Harrison (1972), looking at the character of organisations in general, grouped them into four broad types according to their primary drivers and orientation as set out in Table 10.1.

The organisation in which you work probably does not fall into any one category completely, but some of its dominant character-istics will no doubt be recognisable. Given that much of the work with children and families takes place within a statutory framework, social workers most often find themselves working in organisations which are bureaucratic, and while these have traditionally fitted best into the 'role orientation' described above, the increasing focus in

Table 10.1 Organisational orientation

Organisation type	Characteristics
Power oriented	• Attempts to dominate the internal and external environment
	• Managed through absolute control over subordinates
	• Little attention to human values and welfare
	• Competitive
	• Driven by struggle for personal advantage
Role oriented	• Bureaucratic
	• Emphasis on legality, legitimacy and responsibility
	• Conflict regulated by rules and procedures
	• Rights and privileges defined and adhered to
	• Emphasis on hierarchy and status
	• Predictable, stable and respectable
Task oriented	• Structures, functions and activities all focused on organisational goals
	• Dominated by task accomplishment
	• Individuals trained to perform task competently or replaced
	• Authority derived from appropriate knowledge and competence
	• Rapid and flexible organisation
	• Collaboration to promote goal achievement
People oriented	• Exists to serve the needs of the members
	• Authority only occasionally assigned by task competence
	• Influence through individual example and helpfulness
	• Decision-making using consensus methods
	• Roles assigned by personal preference
	• Focus on individual need for learning and growth

professional development on competence and the emphasis through audit on performance indicators and outputs may well see organisations beginning to migrate towards a greater 'task orientation'. For example, in the task-oriented organisation described above, collaboration is a characteristic employed to promote goal achievement, and certainly multi-agency working and greater coordination of services for children is now a central tenet of government policy. However, it is interesting to note that in an American study of the coordination of services offered to children by 32 public service offices, Glisson and

Hemmelgarn (1998) found that inter-organisational coordination *per se* had a negative effect on service quality and no effect on outcomes for the children they served.

In working with children and families, the wider environment is always a clear focus of attention, and it may be useful to remember that organisations are themselves situated within communities, with the reputation and local 'standing' of the agency likely to have an impact on how you feel and indeed how you are perceived by others – service users and professionals. This was well illustrated by an experienced care manager taking part in a pilot project with carers in general practitioner (GP) surgeries, evaluated by one of the authors. The care manager was seconded to the GP surgery from the local social services office for one day each week. In her substantive post with social services, she was used to being greeted on the telephone with a certain ambivalence or lack of interest in her offers of help, and so she was shocked to find that by simply announcing herself as coming from the GP surgery, she could 'feel people standing to attention' at the other end of the telephone. She also reported a real temptation to adopt a different telephone voice for her surgery 'persona'.

Culture

Culture can be thought of as the social glue of the organisation. As well as being influenced by structures and strategies, the environment in which you work will also depend on 'shared ways of seeing, thinking and doing' which can be termed collectively as the organisational culture, variously expressed as follows:

> how things get done around here

> values and expectations which organisation members come to share

> the social glue that holds the organisation together

> the taken for granted and shared meanings that people assign to their social surroundings. (Hawkins and Shohet 2006, p.168)

Depending on your standpoint, culture can be viewed as something that an organisation 'has', which can be changed or imposed by management or, it can be seen as what the organisation 'is', a summation of the ideas, beliefs and values of those who make up the organisation (Thompson *et al.* 1996). Whichever is the dominant approach will have a profound effect on your experience of working in a particular agency.

Lysons (1997) likened culture to an iceberg, which we have represented in the form of a triangle in Figure 10.1.

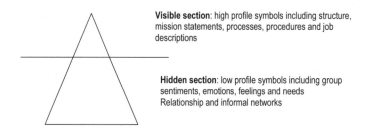

Visible section: high profile symbols including structure, mission statements, processes, procedures and job descriptions

Hidden section: low profile symbols including group sentiments, emotions, feelings and needs Relationship and informal networks

Figure 10.1 Visible and hidden aspects of organisational culture

Figure 10.1 shows that what is most noticeable about culture is the high profile symbols, designed to communicate ideas and assumptions to the external as well as the internal world through such things as prestige buildings or events, logos and mission statements. However, of more significance to those *inside* the organisation are the low profile symbols, such as the day-to-day practice experiences of workers and service users and carers, the use of particular language or jargon, how meetings are called and by whom, and the ways in which decisions are made, communicated and implemented. In many instances, there can be a dissonance between the high profile and low profile symbols. For example, an organisation may have an impressive policy about the key importance of ongoing professional development, yet fail to provide the backfill and release arrangements that translate that policy into a practical reality for frontline staff, as one newly qualified social worker noted.

❝ Yes, most definitely. The agency are committed to it [the PQ framework], yes, they can do the financial bit, but in terms of all the other things – mentoring, support, release and backfill – well, it's just not there. (NQSW) **❞**

Organisations are composed of people, and organisational behaviours, attitudes and values are therefore dependent on the beliefs held by individual members. A healthy culture depends on how well individual beliefs and motivations are aligned with those of the organisation. Again, this interrelationship will not be a static one, and Figure 10.2 uses the iceberg analogy to represent stages in breakdown, if the organisational culture loses its integrity and becomes fractured. Which of the diagrams best portrays the current position of your organisation?

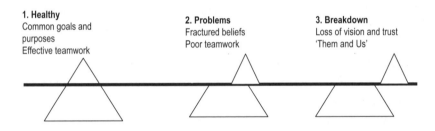

1. Healthy
Common goals and purposes
Effective teamwork

2. Problems
Fractured beliefs
Poor teamwork

3. Breakdown
Loss of vision and trust
'Them and Us'

Figure 10.2 Aligned and fractured cultures (adapted from Thody *et al.* 2000)

Organisations frequently attempt to deal with the potential for fracture in this way by introducing an overarching philosophy, defining a common purpose, goals and priorities, but the success of this approach will ultimately depend very much on the ownership of the philosophy by all groups. Organisational culture cannot be imposed from above, but must be developed by consultation and participation, and must be relevant to the work at each level within the organisation. This brings us back to an understanding of culture as something that is part of the organisation's *being* rather than something 'handed down from above'.

So far we have assumed that one culture applies in a homogeneous way across the whole organisation whereas in reality culture is often complex and multilayered. For example, different departments or teams within the same organisation may develop a variation or subculture within the corporate 'whole'. These subcultures can have a beneficial effect if they increase a sense of common ownership and purpose within a team, but equally they may result in conflict and tensions. There are a number of dysfunctional cultural dynamics that can all too commonly come to dominate the 'way things are done around here', and each of those identified by Hawkins and Shohet (2006) is worth a brief mention.

BLAME

This type of culture is rooted in seeking out and blaming individual failings for what are in truth organisational difficulties. Managers with this mindset deny or marginalise the significance of the organisation's contribution to any dysfunction, stress or conflict, preferring to identify a difficult or problematic person, who if they cannot be brought into line, might need to be removed. Scapegoating like this can happen at every level in an organisation, and even within a team, in the belief that efficiency can be regained if only the problem person can be sorted out. The real danger of accepting this culture is that, in attempting to avoid being identified as the 'problem person', you end up denying your own needs for support and become stifled by secrecy, attempting to 'struggle on alone'.

BUREAUCRATIC EFFICIENCY

Bureaucracy frequently comes to dominate an organisational culture as a defence against anxiety, which is a particular problem in social work with children and families, which involves high levels of uncertainty and risk. Safe and effective performance in children's services is guided by rules about who is authorised to make certain decisions, and it is appropriate to have processes aimed at ensuring that no one person is left in isolation, holding sole responsibility. While there is much in the bureaucratic process that is therefore potentially helpful, you need to remain guarded about allowing the structures to become either too rigidly applied or too loose and chaotic. For example, assessment systems used to identify needs and match them to resources can reduce complex issues to oversimplistic categories, narrowing your professional autonomy and any chance of a creative response to service users' problems. This sort of culture is likely to be characterised by a problem-centred approach, tightly bound with policies, procedures and documentation for every eventuality, and focused almost exclusively on task completion.

COMPETITION

Although it is at odds with many of the core values of social work, competition is a common feature of working within almost any organisation these days. Not only is the organisation itself likely to be engaging in competition with others for resources, but also there will be groups, subgroups, rivalries and personality clashes in the pursuit of resources, power and influence *within* the organisation. Hierarchical organisations are particularly prone to a culture of competition, which can also take on greater significance for staff in organisations that are undergoing change and reorganisation, with the attendant threat of redeployment or redundancy.

CRISIS

An organisation driven by crisis can be recognised by the lack of priority given to the creation and maintenance of uninterrupted time for reflection and forward planning. Practice in this culture is dominated by 'the moment', in which ad hoc responses and decision-making in a hurry, before the next deluge, predominates. Where this type of culture prevails, service users soon learn that the best way to get attention is to precipitate a crisis, thus establishing a self-perpetuating cycle.

ADDICTION

Finally, there is an organisational culture which can be viewed through the metaphor of addiction. It is possible for the organisation itself to behave like an addictive substance, producing 'workaholism' in particular individuals, who forsake any sustainable work/life balance as their 'addiction' overtakes them. Faced with an addicted member, others within the team or management tier either collude or develop a co-dependency. Although mostly covert, this culture delivers the message that to forgo breaks and to work late is 'the way things are done around here'.

Climate

Structure and culture combine together to create a climate, which is a reflection of the way that staff *feel* about the organisation for which they are working. Climate has a profound influence on the way in which you engage with the world of work. In a satisfying climate, you will feel able to work with energy and commitment, while dissatisfaction can lead, over time, to distancing and depersonalisation. Climate depends to a large extent on the degree of congruence that exists between how you want to practise and your perception of what is needed or demanded of you by the agency. You may already be aware of the depth to which any areas of mismatch can influence your attitude to work.

Importantly, organisational climate has been shown to be a significant predictor of both the quality and outcomes of services for children, with improvements in psychosocial functioning significantly greater for children serviced by offices with more positive climates (Glisson and Hemmelgarn 1998). This study looked at several aspects of the workplace to assess the quality of the organisational climate, and you might find it interesting to consider the statements in Box 10.1 in relation to your own workplace.

How far do the areas of strong disagreement, where you have scored 4 or 5, represent areas of mismatch between the requirements of the job and personal principle? It is possible to become caught up in the organisation's own conflicting values which often reflect a discrepancy between the lofty 'mission statement' and the daily experience of work. What steps could you take, individually, or along with your supervisor, manager or team, to improve the areas of 'strong disagreement' or person/job mismatch?

Becoming an effective organisational operator

Managing conflict

There is no doubt that social work can be a stressful job, and some of that stress will inevitably be caused by conflict, not only with service users but also with colleagues, supervisors and managers. Recognising that conflict is a normal part of everyday life is a helpful starting point, and the experience need not be entirely negative. Positive outcomes such as improved relationships and personal development can emerge,

---

Box 10.1 Assessing the organisational climate

What sort of climate are you currently working in? Record your response to each of the statements below by ticking one box in each row and adding up the total scores (1 = strongly agree, 5 = strongly disagree):

	1	2	3	4	5
My agency treats me fairly	☐	☐	☐	☐	☐
My role is clearly defined	☐	☐	☐	☐	☐
I have sufficient time to complete my tasks each day	☐	☐	☐	☐	☐
I balance care and control well within my role	☐	☐	☐	☐	☐
Cooperation with other agencies is good	☐	☐	☐	☐	☐
My professional development is encouraged	☐	☐	☐	☐	☐
Job satisfaction here is high	☐	☐	☐	☐	☐
Emotional exhaustion is low	☐	☐	☐	☐	☐
I experience high levels of personal accomplishment	☐	☐	☐	☐	☐
Practice is always client centred	☐	☐	☐	☐	☐
Totals	☐	☐	☐	☐	☐

A low score overall (< 30) indicates an organisation which provides a positive climate for staff; higher scores (> 31) indicate a more negative climate.

---

although inappropriate responses such as violence and aggression must never be tolerated. In these hopefully extreme circumstances, you should turn to the agency's safety policy if the difficulties are with service users, or to the harassment and bullying at work policies if you are experiencing problems with colleagues or managers.

Since it is largely unavoidable, the important issue is how you respond to conflict when it does arise. Five 'styles' of response to conflict are commonly identified from research (Hughes and Wearing 2007, p.105):

- *integrating*: a collaborative style that seeks to maximise advantages for both parties

- *compromising*: both parties give some ground to resolve the issue

- *obliging*: one person denies their own interests to be acceding to the other's position

- *avoiding*: one party withdraws from the conflict and consequently the other's position prevails

- *forcing*: one party forces their interests to be accepted at the expense of the other's.

You may have experienced one or all of these styles at different times in your working life, but an integrating style would appear to fit most comfortably with social work values and to have the greatest chance of success in reducing disruption in the workplace. It is also noticeable that the three principal formal processes for conflict resolution, namely negotiation, mediation and arbitration, all incorporate an integrating style. The particular value of negotiation is that, by paying attention to both the substance of the disagreement and the relationship of the parties involved, resolution can be achieved in such a way that neither party feels that they are the losers. Negotiation is based on four principles (Lens 2004):

1. *Separate the person from the problem*: Hold back from blame in order to create a positive working relationship, recognising that emotions and hurt feelings can become part of the equation.

2. *Focus on interests not positions*: Take a step back to look for any common interests, as a focus for consideration, through which the parties can be brought together in active and more purposeful dialogue.

3. *Consider options for mutual gain*: View the situation from a number of perspectives and look for different solutions each with the other party's interests in mind.

4. *Use objective criteria*: Try to define some criteria as headings under which to consider options, actions and outcomes. Procedural fairness is important and identifying agreed criteria in the process can help to ensure that decisions are based not on a battle of wills but on an evaluation of 'best fit' given the particular circumstances.

As a general rule, it is always best to try to resolve disagreements directly with those concerned by informal discussion at the lowest possible level within the organisational hierarchy.

Assessing teamwork

Social workers most often work in teams, and in Chapter 8 we looked at teams from the point of view of support, considering some of the roles and stages in their formation. Now that you have had some time to observe its workings at close quarters, it might be opportune to review some of the characteristics of your own team, making an assessment of its effectiveness and your own contribution to the quality of teamwork by completing the questionnaire about effective teamwork in Box 10.2.

Box 10.2 Assessing effective teamwork

Think of a team of which you are a part. Using a scale of 1–10, where 1 is low and 10 is high, score each statement to reflect your opinion of the quality of the teamwork of which you are a part.

		Score
Purpose and direction	We have a sense of purpose	
	We know where we are going	
Communication	We communicate well within the team	
	We know what is going on in other teams	
Decision-making	We make clear, timely decisions	
	We act on decisions when agreed	
Participation	I am involved in policy/organisation issues	
	I am supported and monitored in my work	
Openness and trust	I feel comfortable to speak openly	
	We can disagree without difficulty	
Use of time	We use our time together well	
	We focus on important issues	
Tasks	We share tasks fairly	
	Tasks are allocated to match interests and abilities	
Flexibility	We plan ahead to be ready for change	
	We can be flexible to meet different situations	
Evaluation	We review progress regularly	
	We reflect critically on our work	

In the areas that you did not score highly, can you identify any significant barriers?

Source: adapted from Thody *et al.* (2000)

Most social workers place great value on their teams and feel supported by them, but that is not to say that defensive or negative attitudes might not develop from time to time, and in these circumstances it is important to try to understand why individuals are feeling as they do. More commonly, teamwork can be thwarted by a number of organisational barriers. For instance, if a group is larger than six to eight people, fully collaborative work is less easy, and it might be a good idea to delegate a smaller subgroup to undertake a specific task on behalf of the larger group. Work overload, resulting in tasks not being completed, little time for review, and unfair allocation of responsibilities, may also undermine teamwork, as can a lack of leadership or organisational change, both of which can result in a lack of purpose, direction and participation, as well as poor decision-making and review. Management texts and handbooks abound in which it is acknowledged as a general truth that the key to a successful organisation is effective teamwork. However, the complexities of working in a team should never be underestimated. Skills in teamwork are rarely part of professional training or induction, and are something that you are more likely to be expected to pick up as you go along, almost by osmosis, as you might learn the skills of being a parent.

According to Belbin (2004), a 'super team' composed entirely of clever people does not guarantee effectiveness. He showed that critical thinkers tended to be 'critical' in both senses of the word and, faced with a problem, found a large number of more negative things to say which preoccupied their time in endless thinking, discussing and debating, while also alienating other members of the team socially, and interfering with the integration and general cohesion of the group. Although proposing and opposing – playing devil's advocate – are important processes in team decisions, there are other equally important aspects which cannot be neglected if the team is to be an effective one. Gathering resources, collecting and organising information, recording current knowledge, and coordinating plans and actions are all equally important activities. All of this points to the necessity for a broad skills 'mix' and completing the questionnaire above might help you to assess the quality of the teamwork in which you are involved. If team members have sufficient courage, it might be informative for a whole group to complete the exercise and discuss their assessments with one another.

Accountability

Being accountable is one of the key differences identified by newly qualified social workers as they move from student to employee, and is responsible for much of the 'thud' associated with the arrival of professional status discussed in Part I. There are four broad dimensions of organisational accountability (Corbett 1991), as illustrated in Figure 10.3.

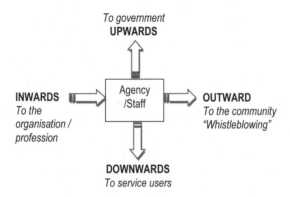

Figure 10.3 Organisational accountabilities

Accountability for social workers is multiplied by the number of different 'constituencies' which hold social work to account, of which Banks (2002) identifies four forms:

- *technical accountability*: related to knowledge about what works and skills in how to do things

- *procedural accountability*: set out in regulations, guidance and agency procedures

- *managerial accountability*: – in response to orders or requests from organisational managers

- *ethical accountability*: based on values, codes of conduct and personal understandings of what is right and wrong.

Deciding how to combine and manage these different forms of accountability understandably presents a confusing picture for newly qualified workers, although codes of practice produced by the social care councils in England, Northern Ireland, Scotland and Wales provide guidelines for ensuring professionally accountable standards, and Lord Laming (2009) recommended in his report on the protection of children in England that these should be revised and strengthened by statute.

Performance measurement is closely linked to accountability, but difficulties arise if 'outcomes' turn out to be process measures that emphasise the quantity of what was provided over any consideration of its quality. It has been shown that improved 'outputs', such as availability, responsiveness and information-sharing, do not necessarily equate to improved outcomes for children (Glisson and Hemmelgarn 1998; Scottish Executive 2002). Although these matters are likely to be of greater concern to your manager, in relation to the service overall, monitoring the quality of your own performance, and keeping a record as part of your personal development plan, can also be a worthwhile activity, perhaps incorporating feedback from service users, carers, other professionals, and agencies, to develop your understanding of what is key in defining the quality of what you are providing.

Key considerations for working in a satisfying climate

Drawing on the work of Charles and Butler (2004), you might find the following checklist helpful in identifying a number of practical ways in which you can contribute to the development of a satisfying climate:

- Build professional credibility by attending to self-image. Professional credibility is established by very simple actions such as being organised, punctual, having a clutter-free desk and producing concise and timely reports. Positioned as someone whose organisational abilities and time-management skills are exemplary, you may find a greater willingness to listen to you when you need to say no to additional work or inappropriate tasks.

- Take control of your professional development. Think about linking your preferences for development to any 'skill shortages' or specific niches in the team, group or agency, developing yourself as a resource on which colleagues can depend.

- Accept that hierarchical organisations are frequently limited in the ways in which they work with emotion. In these circumstances it is vital to use personnel procedures to look after yourself, by planning and taking your full leave entitlement, taking time off in lieu when you have worked additional hours, and taking sick leave when appropriate.

- Avoid conspiracy theory as a way of understanding agency decision-making, and accept contradictions as a reflection of organisational complexity (e.g. where some of the intentions set out in a mission statement are not delivered in practice).

- Taking a self-critical, flexible and adaptive stance will maximise your capacity, albeit at the micro-level, to influence organisational change.

Chapter 11

Managing Increasing Complexity

- Building on critical reflection
- Leadership and being led
- The learning organisation
- Key considerations in managing increasing complexity

In this chapter we explore some of the links between critical reflection, reflective practice and the learning organisation, as you develop your professional identity and take on increasingly complex work. Gould and Baldwin (2004, p.4) have linked reflective learning with the learning organisation through a discussion of three models of problem-solving. First, as presented in Chapter 1, we know that professionals draw on formal knowledge and research to guide their interventions, but their strategies for problem-solving are derived from a set of individual, situational rules developed from experience in the workplace over time. Second, practice which is generally understood simply as applied formal knowledge pays insufficient attention to the influence that context has on how knowledge is put to use. Despite widespread references to skill transfer as a core competence in social work, there is evidence to show that practice knowledge is actually very context specific, so the successful transfer of learning cannot take place without some reworking and adaptation. Third, 'the problem' itself is a matter of interpretation, depending on the context, in contrast to 'rule-based' approaches to practice where there is an assumption that there are problem types to which predetermined solutions can then be applied.

These core premises of the development of professional practice have strong synergy with those of the learning organisation, in which learning is understood to be ongoing and embedded in the organisational context. In other words, learning not only takes place when attending a course or undertaking formal training, but also occurs in the workplace, often in informal and unplanned ways, and on a continuing basis.

Building on critical reflection

Decision-making and uncertainty

In Chapters 1 and 2 we considered the development of professional expertise through the transformation of context-free rules into your own repertoire of situational rules, applied to an increasing range of practice situations, and informed by overarching and underpinning knowledge intertwined with each other in increasingly complex and creative ways. Decision-making or professional judgement can therefore be seen to call for an active synthesis of the components at the corners of the triangle in Figure 11.1, while also responding to the uniqueness, complexity and uncertainty of each individual situation. Managing these dynamic tensions draws on many of your graduate skills, and is the very antithesis of the application of the rigid mechanistic procedures associated with 'new managerialism'.

Figure 11.1 Developing judgement and decision-making

Decision-making in social work is generally understood to follow a rational approach, assuming that people act in a logical, linear way, choosing options that bring the highest returns for the least costs. This focus on rational choices fits well with evidence-based approaches to practice based as they are on the quasi-scientific selection and evaluation of different courses of action. The decision-making process can be divided into a number of stages in which the problem is defined, alternatives generated and selected according to available information, action implemented and then followed up by monitoring and evaluation of the results. The whole process becomes a repeating cycle, with new problems defined according to evaluation of the outcomes of previous decisions.

However, this description represents a rather idealised version of how decisions are actually reached in practice, as a response from a social worker in our own study reveals.

> **"** I can honestly say, since qualifying ... I haven't looked at a single paper, a single piece of research. In the field, well it's very limited ... you don't have the range of journals available to you ... and more importantly, it's time. (Social worker – 6 months post-qualification) **"**

The everyday experience of decision-making for most social workers is more likely to be messier and more unpredictable than that outlined above, constrained by factors such as a lack of information, the degree of complexity of the problems faced, the limited capacity of individuals to process information, the short time-frames within which a decision is required, and conflict between different goals. What is needed in these circumstances is the capacity to live with and to tolerate a significant degree of ambiguity and even paradox. The world does not divide easily into what is unambiguously 'good' for children and what is not, what is safe and what is not. The truth is often that we do not know, and that it really does 'all depend'. In *War and Peace*, Tolstoy included some wonderful descriptions about how battles which look very clear to historians with the benefit of hindsight never actually seem that way to those in the heat of the battle. These passages were meant as a metaphor for society, to show that there is seldom a vantage point from which it is possible to get the full picture in the here and now.

French (2001) quotes Keats, who coined the term 'negative capability' to describe a state in which a person is 'capable of being in uncertainties, mysteries, doubts, without any irritable reaching after fact and reason'. His 'negative capability' is the ability to stick with the sometimes frightening fact that in certain situations we simply do not know. Where negative capability fails, your energies get 'dispersed' in one of three ways, through explanation, emotional reaction or physical action. These reactions may be very familiar to you, either as part of your own responses to complex and uncertain situations, or as behaviours that you have seen in others, at work or elsewhere. Negative capability describes the capacity to tolerate the emotional impact of the uncertainties and doubts that professional life can throw up. Developing negative capability means that you are able to stay with the moment, to wait, holding tensions and anxieties, living with problems that may be intractable, accepting paradoxes and dilemmas for what they are, conserving and preserving your energies to discover a new thought, idea or possibility for more meaningful, positive action (French 2001).

Reflection on and in action

Part of this vital ability to 'stay with the moment' is developed and strengthened through the practice of reflection. As a student social worker, you will have been required to produce written reflections on your practice to demonstrate to a variety of assessors that you were developing the insight and awareness needed to become a qualified social worker. As a qualified professional, however, reflection is no longer about evidence for others, but rather a means by which you choose to develop your practice *for yourself*, so that you are comfortable and secure in the ideas and approaches that inform your own decision-making.

Reflection can be broken down into two separate, but linked, components. Reflection *on* action is focused on thinking about what you have already done, in order to inform what you will do in the future. Table 11.1 provides a framework for thinking about this type of reflection.

Table 11.1 Framework for reflection on action

Answer the following questions in relation to a recent example from your practice.

Description

- Describe the situation, identifying the important issues and participants.

Reflection

- What were you trying to do?
- Why did you take the actions that you did?
- What were the consequences for each participant?
- How did you feel? How did others feel?
- What did they do or say to let you know how they felt?
- How did you show how you were feeling?

Influencing factors

- What internal and external factors influenced your decisions?
- What knowledge and skills did or should have influenced you?
- What should not have influenced you?

Alternatives

- What could you have done differently?
- What other choices could you have made?
- What would have been the consequences of those choices?

Learning

- How can you make sense of this experience, considering both the past and what you could do in the future?
- How do you feel now?
- Have you taken action to support yourself and others as a result of this experience?
- How have you changed?
- Have others changed?
- Is there anything more you need to do as a result? For instance, search out information, undertake some training or reading, etc.

Source: adapted from Johns (1994)

However, reflection is not a process that takes place only after the fact; it also occurs, consciously or not, at the time of the event in question – referred to as reflection *in* action. This type of reflection requires that you metaphorically take a step back from what you are doing *at the time that you are doing* it, disengaging from the 'automatic' part of what you are doing and thinking critically about your practice to make sure that you have paid appropriate attention to every aspect, even as you are actively engaged in the process. Taking these ideas a little further, Barnett (1997) represented three overlapping 'domains' of *critical practice* as shown in Figure 11.2.

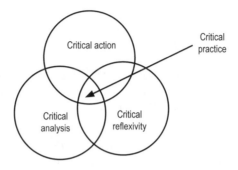

Figure 11.2 The domains of critical practice (after Barnett 1997)

- *Critical analysis* involves the evaluation of knowledge, theories, policies and practice from multiple perspectives, as part of a commitment to ongoing enquiry as you analyse the situation.

- *Critical action* calls for a repertoire of skills, taking account of the context of each situation, working with difference and recognising and challenging power inequalities and structural disadvantage.

- *Critical reflexivity* is about maintaining an aware, reflective and engaged self, questioning personal assumptions and values.

Critical reflexivity, in particular, is a key ingredient in establishing the interactive and circular processes which underpin critical practice, and requires a highly developed sense of self-awareness. The better you know yourself, the more able and open you become to new learning, adapting and developing more flexible and creative approaches to practice, its problems and decision-making dilemmas.

According to Fook and Gardner (2007, p.51), the broad purpose of critical reflection is to 'unsettle the fundamental or dominant thinking implicit in professional practices, in order to see other ways of practising'. It is about unearthing and examining anew your own daily assumptions, including those that may have become lost or obfuscated by internal agency directives. Critical reflection is about finding better ways to practise (action) based on different ways of thinking (analysis). It is the ability to link both aspects of action and analysis that is important.

> **"** But the people who read the papers hate social workers ... so in the end you realise that we're a powerless, oppressed, disadvantaged group of individuals which is quite sad really because you're looking at some superb people. I've never worked with people who care so much and have so many skills. (NQSW) **"**

Practitioners, like the NQSW quoted, often report feeling powerless and lacking in professional autonomy, but taking an active stance and making use of critical reflection, both in and on action, can produce a number of real benefits for your practice.

Leadership and being led

As well as consciously using reflection on and in action to deal with the increasingly complex work that you will be expected to take on as you develop as a professional, the way that colleagues and others do their jobs, particularly those in positions of power within the organisation such as team leaders and managers, will also play an important role in your practice.

Leadership and management are almost 'conjoined twins' in everyday parlance, and certainly there are a number of attributes and skills common to both roles. Management meets the day-to-day requirements for most teams operating in a stable environment, but when conditions become more complex, unpredictable or subject to rapid change, rather more is needed by way of leadership which is creative and focuses on helping the team to cope and continue to function effectively.

Good leadership and management is central to the development of a healthy organisational culture, and although we perhaps no longer believe in the concept of the born leader imbued with heroic qualities, there will be certain key attributes that you use to assess the quality of your leaders or managers, which might include:

- empathy and understanding

- consistency and fairness

- acceptance and respect

- integrity and honesty

- reliability and trustworthiness.

None of these attributes, on its own, is enough to characterise an outstanding leader, but to deliver the full set, consistently and coherently, to a range of different people, certainly requires skills which will take time to develop (see Box 11.1). However, this does not mean that some of the foundations for good leadership skills cannot be laid at the very beginning of your career. In fact, the sooner you start the better. You can begin to develop your own leadership skills by:

- communicating effectively and honestly

- fostering good relationships with others both inside and outside your organisation

- focusing on your own personal and professional development

- developing your critical thinking skills and evidence-based practice so that you are in a position to offer information, advice and support to others

- helping others with problem-solving, planning and getting things done.

Box 11.1 Appraising management skills

Think of the best manager you have ever had:

- How did that person make you feel?
- What skills did that person possess?
- How did they use their skills?

Skills for Care (2008) has produced a leadership and management strategy for social care in England which specifies what managers and leaders need to do, including the following extract:

- Promote and achieve service aims, objectives and goals
- Comply with the Codes of Practice, relevant legislation and agency policies
- Develop partnerships and effective joint and integrated working practices
- Manage resources and budgets effectively
- Manage change effectively
- Manage conflicts and risk effectively
- Inspire staff
- Value people and actively develop talent and potential

Two main themes can be identified from this list – a concern for people and a concern for task. Achieving a balance between these two aspects is a primary focus for managers, both in the day-to-day running of a team, and in some of the more specific aspects of their role, such as supervision. Different permutations of these two themes can be linked to the four leadership styles summarised in Table 11.2, each of which may be familiar to you.

Table 11.2 Leadership styles

Leadership style	Benefits	Disadvantages
Social • Concern for people • No concern for task	Interpersonal skills flourish Good communication Team feels valued	Lack of direction for team Things appear disorganised Not much progresses
Authoritarian • Concern for task • No concern for people	Vision delivered with clarity Well-defined rules, schedules Tasks accomplished	No credit for creativity, difference No room for individual input Blame can become widespread
Impoverished • No concern for people • No concern for task	Minimum interference Team members are free to do what they like	No support Followers feel 'rudderless'
Team • Concern for people • Concern for task	Team highly motivated and valued Tasks accomplished	Can give rise to over-reliance on one individual and personal charisma

The four categories of leadership describe theoretical styles, and provide rather artificial boundaries. If you had to choose one, a leader with a team style, showing concern for people *and* for task might be your preferred option. However, in the real world a successful leader might need to draw on a mix of strategies, according to the circumstances. Sometimes task-achievement must be prioritised, so a more authoritarian approach will be needed, but there will also be times when the team needs to relax, when a more social style will be appropriate. As in much else in life, the key to success lies not in a table of prescribed options, but in the ability to understand the team and its context, and to assess what is necessary to encourage best practice and professional development.

You will also expect a good leader to stand behind the team and support it, as well as getting outside constituencies to support the team's efforts. Leaders need to be able to 'read' and understand others at work effectively, and to use this knowledge to influence them positively to enhance personal as well as organisational objectives. Ahearn *et al.* (2004), in a study of the performance of casework teams in a large state child welfare system in the USA, found that these 'political' skills of leaders explained a significant proportion of the variation in performance between teams.

Having said all that, self-directed teams are beginning to emerge in which a *group* of people have day-to-day responsibility for managing themselves and the work they do. Leadership tasks, for example setting direction or managing conflict, can be taken up by anyone in the group. As individuals accept more responsibility for their work, they also take on a stronger role in leading. Increasingly in team-based organisations, team members also practise some degree of self-management, taking responsibility for the team outcomes by monitoring and managing their own performance as well as helping others to improve their practice.

The learning organisation

The final piece in the jigsaw of managing increasing complexity involves recognising and developing the learning potential of whole organisations.

Managing change

Although a concern for social justice and the social change that necessarily accompanies that goal have long been at the heart of social work practice and values, social workers frequently experience major difficulties when faced with change within their own organisations. While some of these difficulties can be attributed to the ways in which change has occurred, including the often limited extent to which social workers themselves have been involved in the planning, implementation and evaluation processes, others can perhaps be put down to a failure to apply the knowledge and skills that social workers routinely use in helping service users to cope with change. For example, although organisational change often occurs in response to factors external to the organisation, and social workers routinely consider the influence of the wider environment on the well-being of children and families, this knowledge is not necessarily put to good use in coping with changes occurring in their own workplaces. The message here is that you already possess many of the skills needed to participate successfully in the management of organisational change. To take just one example, you will be aware from your own practice experience that it is pointless attempting to change the behaviour of individuals or groups unless they recognise and accept the need for change themselves. The same is true of organisations, sections or teams – the impetus for successful change must come from within. However, even when the need for change has been accepted, managing it will always have an emotional element. Handy (1993) developed a five stage model, set out in Figure 11.3, to chart the emotional impact of change.

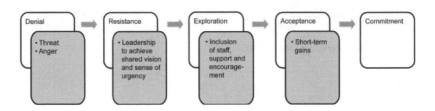

Figure 11.3 Five stage model of change management

The diagram represents the transition from initial feelings of threat and anger, which fuel resistance, through exploration and acceptance, to final commitment. Leadership is needed at each stage: to respond to feelings of threat; to achieve a shared vision; to consult with and include staff at every stage; and to provide encouragement, support and a variety of short-term gains to secure final commitment.

It has been well documented that creating any form of change will meet with resistance which may be rooted in a whole host of factors (Plant 1987):

Fear of the unknown	Lack of or misinformation
Poor relationships	Lack of trust in the organisation
Threat to core skills	Threat to status
Threat to power base	No perceived benefits
Fear of failure	Reluctance to experiment
Strong fixed culture	Reluctance to let go

One of the most influential models of change (Lewin 1952) identifies a three-step process – 'unfreezing', 'moving' and 'refreezing' – in which *unfreezing* involves creating an awareness among stakeholders that change in a system is needed, and the possible methods of achieving it. *Moving* involves choosing one of the methods of change and putting it into action, and after action has taken place, *refreezing* is required in order to consolidate and stabilise the new order.

Later, Lewin borrowed from Newton's Third Law of Motion to develop a technique known as force field analysis, which is used to evaluate organisational change. Newton demonstrated that 'for every action there is an equal and opposite reaction', which, translated into change management theory, means that the more you push for change, the more resistance you will meet. The solution therefore is to stop pushing, and to seek out the cause of the impasse by listing all the forces that are supporting or driving the proposed change on the left hand side of a piece of paper, and all the forces that are resisting or restraining the change on the right hand side. You then look for ways in which the restraining forces can be reduced, and the driving forces increased, in order to shift the equilibrium towards the proposed change.

Lewin's formulation of force field analysis tends to treat resistance as a single state, but other writers (e.g. Fink, Beak and Taddeo 1971) have identified different phases of resistance through which teams and organisations may pass in wrestling with their resistance to change, which we have represented in Figure 11.4.

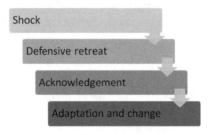

Figure 11.4 Phases of resistance to change

In the *shock* phase, relationships, decision-making and communication become confused and frozen, leading to *defensive retreat*. Teams and their members withdraw into a constrained mode of operation with rigidly applied procedures and autocratic decision-making. Once the need for things to change has been *acknowledged*, more confrontation is experienced but support also develops, so that when the final stage – *adaptation and change* – is reached, communication is wider, more open and trusting, and a willingness to experiment creatively with different ways of working is adopted.

The message here is therefore that, just because you have worked through the options and devised what you think is a good solution, it does not follow that others will accept it without the opportunity to go through their own thinking processes.

As noted by Hawkins and Shohet (2006):

> it can be counter-productive to give people your marvellous scenarios for their future. They need to be involved in the thinking through and planning changes so that they have the opportunity to react, then understand the need for change, and then adapt to the future necessities. (Hawkins and Shohet 2006, p.187)

Learning teams

Whereas in Chapter 10 we described culture as the 'social glue' of organisations, there is a sense in which learning can be viewed as the 'professional glue' that is also essential for binding an organisation together. No doubt part of your motivation for choosing a social work career was to have the opportunity to learn new things, to acquire new skills and to play a part in developing new knowledge.

Using learning as a 'tool' and central theme with which to bind disparate organisational units together is an idea drawn from those associated with the concept of the 'learning organisation'. Gould (2000) discussed ways in which these ideas, originally based in business management theory, might be translated into strategies for the development of social work practice by focusing on the team as the primary context for learning, which supports a reflective cycle of action that becomes part of everyday, professional activity. Teams have the possibility to learn and recreate themselves, to set challenging new goals and to be self-directive and reflective, thinking insightfully together about complex issues (Lick 2006). In this way, learning, training and development are not discrete and separate from practice but rather fully integrated with it. We have seen that social workers place high value on members of their teams, as well as on learning and development, and it would not be difficult for you to identify a number of team-based activities that could be translated into primary learning opportunities including, for instance:

- presentations to team meetings

- sharing learning from external events

- co-working with colleagues

- joint working with internal and external partners

- sharing between teams through informal contacts

- workshops and seminars

- secondments across the agency and with partner organisations.

The Social Care Institute for Excellence (SCIE 2004) has identified five areas in which the characteristics of a learning organisation can be demonstrated, and it might be interesting for you to use the answers to the following questions to gauge the stage of development of your own agency as a learning organisation.

ORGANISATIONAL STRUCTURE

- *Service user and carer feedback and participation*: How well is this sought, resourced and used to inform practice?

- *Teamworking*: How well does your agency make use of different staff skills?

- *Collaboration*: How collaborative or 'parallel' is partnership working?

ORGANISATIONAL CULTURE

- *Shared vision*: How are beliefs, values, goals and objectives communicated?

- *Creativity*: Are new ideas and methods encouraged?

- *Learning*: Are you encouraged to learn from mistakes or test out new ideas?

- *Research*: Are messages and evidence from research considered and used in practice?

INFORMATION SYSTEMS

- *Effective information systems*: How effectively can you use systems for internal and external communication?

- *Policies and procedures*: How accessible, meaningful and understood are these?

HUMAN RESOURCE PRACTICES

- *Continuous development*: How clear are the supervision and appraisal policies?

LEADERSHIP

- *Organisational change and service development:* What capacity is there for development and change beyond day-to-day delivery?

Learning organisations challenge individuals to look at their own work and role more broadly, to develop their knowledge and skills for the benefit of all, rather than avoiding change, stagnating and taking refuge 'in a rut'. The organisation that learns then develops its own irresistible forward momentum, in which the whole workforce has an investment.

Practitioner 'knowledge bank'

Another important element from learning organisation theory which could enhance the workplace culture is the value accorded to the practice knowledge held by practitioners (Gould 2000), which is often unacknowledged. Recognising and recording its existence, actively building an agency 'knowledge bank' and promoting it as a practice resource within and between teams (as well as with senior managers) could provide a further mechanism through which different elements of the organisation become 'networked', so that cohesion and communication, horizontally between peers and hierarchically between levels, is enhanced.

Key considerations in managing increasing complexity

Drawing on the work of Clarke and Stewart (1997), you might find the following suggestions helpful in developing a critically reflective response to problems that seem tricky and resistant to resolution:

- Instead of searching for certainty, try to accept that your understanding will be partial and foster your ability to tolerate not knowing.

- Limiting yourself to thinking in a linear way might mean that you miss the important dynamic interrelationships that a more holistic approach can reveal.

- Accept different perspectives and approaches. You do not have to be constrained by the obvious or conventional and limit your practice to 'the way things have always been done around here'.

- Draw in as wide an array of opinions and interests as possible and be open to 'outsiders' and their new attitudes, ideas and perspectives.

- Spread your net as wide as possible and consult not just the usual people with the usual answers. Be prepared to learn from experiment, innovation and creativity.

Chapter **12**

Moving Forward: Continuing Professional Development

- :* Lifelong learning and CPD
- :* The framework: PDPs, PRTL and PQ
- :* Managing your pathway
- :* Key considerations for successful continuing professional development

Towards the end of your first year in practice, you will be ready to review the progress you have made, reflecting on all of the changes that have taken place in a relatively short time, as well as looking forward to plan the next steps in your career. In this chapter, we consider some of the structures and frameworks that might inform your planning, so that you are ready to meet the challenges of new or more complex work, and to take full advantage of opportunities for your professional development.

Lifelong learning and CPD

According to the Children's Workforce Development Council (CWDC 2006), continuing professional development can be defined as an on-going, planned learning and development process which:

- enables workers to expand and fulfil their potential

- contributes to work-based and personal development

- can be applied or assessed against competencies and organisational performance

- includes any activity that increases knowledge, experience and understanding, improves performance and contributes to lifelong learning.

Lifelong learning is a concept which has taken root not only because it is important to people in general to maintain and develop their mental capital and well-being (Department for Innovation, Universities and Skills (DIUS) 2008), but also because knowledge can rapidly become obsolescent. If you do not continually grasp opportunities to develop, you do not just get stuck in a rut and stagnate, you actually move backwards. Social work is almost continually facing new challenges as a result of changes in legislation and regulation, the way work is structured and organised, and the implementation of new technologies.

You could think of your training as having provided you with an initial road map with which to start your journey. You are making decisions in the field, drawing on knowledge and skills according to the surrounding territory, rather like a map-reader (Cooper 2008). The ultimate aim of continuing professional development (CPD) is to enable you to move from map-reader to map-maker, drawing more and more on the 'graduateness' of an inquiring and independent mind.

You will already be familiar with the idea of competence and occupational standards from your training, and CPD in social work is similarly based on a variety of competency frameworks which specify certain standards, outcomes and indicators. Rather than getting bogged down by the prescriptive nature of these competency frameworks, a better idea is to regard them as 'activity structures' which help you as a new practitioner to familiarise yourself with some of the current priorities of the profession and its jargon, to provide higher education institutions with ways to make assessments for credit within academic awards, and to assist organisations to articulate standards aimed at limiting risk and protecting themselves from 'mistakes' in practice.

In 2006, the CWDC, together with Skills for Care and other partner agencies, developed a CPD strategy and framework for social care in England in which they promote a 'whole systems' approach, integrating the needs of individual staff with those of the organisation, creating some of the preconditions for creating the 'learning organisations' that we considered in Chapter 11. Indeed, the codes of conduct of the care councils for the four UK countries specify that employers must provide training and development opportunities to enable workers to strengthen and develop their knowledge and skills, and although these are not yet mandatory, Lord Laming's 2009 report on the protection of children in England has recommended an urgent move in that direction so, at the time of writing, further change is actively under consideration.

At a personal level, the essential elements of the whole systems approach for you will be:

- a personal development plan, linked to your job description, occupational standards and other relevant competencies

- access to development activities and relevant qualifications

- appraisal linked to your personal development plan

- a CPD portfolio – either paper or electronic.

Line managers have a key role to play here, and your agency should have a clear CPD framework in place, with the infrastructure to support learning and systems for tracking the CPD achievements of staff. Although you will probably need to take the initiative in planning, seeking out and suggesting specific activities, there is a clear expectation and responsibility on your employer to make an active contribution to supporting and guiding you in your career development. The primary mechanism for linking personal development and organisational requirements will be your personal development plan.

The frameworks: PDPs, PRTL and PQ

Personal development plans (PDPs)

Chapter 4 suggested a cyclical five stage process for personal development planning. If you have been following the process, you should be about ready now to tackle Stage 5 – reviewing and revising the plan – as part of your annual appraisal and performance management process.

Because the whole plan is drawn up around your chosen set of professional standards (e.g. NQSW programme outcomes; PQ consolidation module learning outcomes) your PDP will automatically make the links between your learning and that of the team and the organisation, as recommended in the CWDC CPD strategy. The summary checklist in Box 12.1 is a reminder of the process, and for the purposes of this chapter, the last two prompts are important.

Box 12.1 Personal development planning process: summary checklist

Reviewing the cycle:

- Has my initial self-assessment been discussed in supervision?

- What learning objectives, linked to professional standards, have been agreed?

- Am I clear about the timetable?

- Am I clear about which areas have been prioritised and what I need to do to meet each objective?

- Am I clear about what evidence is needed and how it will be recorded and stored?

- Are there any useful links to be made with extracts from my reflexive journal?

- Will what I am going to do contribute to PRTL?

- Will what I am going to do contribute to evidence for a PQ award?

Post-registration training and learning (PRTL)

The key principles underpinning PRTL (e.g. GSCC 2006b) can be summarised as follows:

- PRTL is the registrant's responsibility.

- PRTL does not need to be a difficult or time-consuming task.

- PRTL should be the outcome of learning and development activities that both you and your employer recognise.

- PRTL is intended to provide service users, colleagues and potential employers with evidence that you are competent to remain on the register.

- PRTL is a flexible process to allow scope for recognition of your individual achievements and to help raise standards.

Post-registration training and learning is a key condition for continued registration as a professional social worker, and your employer must have a mechanism for recording and tracking all CPD activities undertaken by the qualified social workers they employ. This means that there should be a clear agency policy, with mechanisms in supervision, team meetings and formal appraisal to monitor requirements. In our own study, we found that where there are formal external drivers for particular requirements, policies and procedures are much more likely to be in place to support activity. This was certainly the case with PRTL, so it is important that you familiarise yourself with your own agency's specific arrangements.

Each of the four UK countries has developed slightly different approaches to the specific requirements. Full details are available on the websites of each of the care councils involved but a very short synopsis is given in Table 12.1.

Table 12.1 Requirements for PRTL across the four UK countries

UK country	Minimum requirement for PRTL
England General Social Care Council (GSCC)	• All social workers must undertake 90 hours or 15 days of PRTL to be evidenced at point of re-registration • PQ awards can be used as evidence but are not a specific requirement
Northern Ireland Northern Ireland Social Care Council (NISCC)	• By 2010, PRTL will be linked to agreed accredited training and/or qualifications
Scotland Scottish Social Services Council (SSSC)	• NQSWs must complete 24 days (144 hours) within the first 12 months of which 5 days must focus on working with colleagues and other professionals to identify, assess and manage risk to vulnerable people • Re-registration must take place on or before 14-month anniversary • Thereafter, 15 days over 3 years, of which 5 days must focus on working with colleagues and other professionals to identify, assess and manage risk to vulnerable people
Wales Care Council for Wales (CCW)	• All social workers must undertake 90 hours or 15 days of PRTL to be evidenced at point of re-registration • PQ awards can be used as evidence but are not a specific requirement

Source: adapted from SWAP (2009)

The registration rules specify that every social worker must take individual responsibility for keeping a record of the post-registration training and learning they have undertaken, and that failure to meet this condition may be treated as misconduct. Your record of achievement can be kept as a paper file or electronically and there are exemplars and guidance on each of the care councils' websites as well as some suggestions already made in Chapter 4.

The *type* of activities that will meet the requirements are not necessarily specified in detail by each care council, in recognition of the fact that social work takes place in a wide range of settings and contexts. It is worth bearing in mind that the time requirements for PRTL apply equally to all social workers, regardless of the actual number of contracted hours of employment. The time does not have to be made up of full days, but can be a mix of short and longer periods of learning and training. Nor does it have to be spread evenly over the period of registration, so that your planning can be flexible to meet your own particular needs and circumstances.

However, you are expected to choose training, learning and development activities that you have undertaken which:

- benefit your current employment

- benefit your career progression

- reflect your preferred learning style

- make the most of the learning opportunities available to you as part of your wider professional development.

Again, it is important that there is a clear and unambiguous link integrating your plans for, and recording of, PRTL requirements with your agency's arrangements for tracking continuing professional development. As explored in some detail in Chapter 9, supervision provides a good opportunity for you to:

- discuss PRTL with your manager

- identify areas for your personal development, linked to your PDP

- identify the learning opportunities that your agency can provide or to which access can be facilitated for you.

If you are self-employed, you will still need to satisfy the relevant care council that you have taken part in post-registration training and learning when you renew your registration.

Post-qualifying (PQ) frameworks

PRTL fits within the broader post-qualifying (PQ) frameworks for social work education and training. These aim to create opportunities for training and learning that can be:

- flexible, allowing for individual circumstances and aspirations

- a shared responsibility for you and your manager, with learning and development achieved through a range of routes that have equal value and can incorporate

  ◦ individual training needs

  ◦ an employment-based focus

  ◦ a policy-based focus.

As part of a wider framework of PQ qualifications, the post-registration training and learning that we have considered above can be achieved through any combination of the following three different 'modes' of learning.

INFORMAL LEARNING AND PRACTICE DEVELOPMENT

Although by no means an exhaustive list, you might draw on secondment or shadowing the work of a colleague in a related team or profession; undertaking a piece of research related to an issue raised in your practice; learning from reflection on a particular case or activity; taking on new or challenging tasks or responsibilities; giving a presentation; leading a discussion; or running a seminar or group.

UNASSESSED COURSES AND TRAINING

These more formal programmes, probably taking you away from the workplace for a specified number of days, include in-house training (e.g. specialist training about children in care, or approved training in child protection).

CERTIFICATED AND ASSESSED LEARNING, THROUGH A HIGHER EDUCATION INSTITUTION

Although these courses of study may be increasingly delivered wholly by distance learning or a blend of web-based and attendance days, this will generally be much more like the formal study that you experienced as a full-time student. It will carry academic credits and lead to a named award. However, to fit within a professional development framework, there will always be a focus on the assessment of your professional practice through written evidence of your 'capability', and a variety of observations and reports of practice from others (social workers or other professionals with whom you work) to confirm 'performance'.

Variations in PQ framework requirements

Again, in developing specific requirements for a formal PQ framework, the four UK countries have taken different approaches, and some of the more important aspects of each are summarised in Table 12.2 (Social Policy and Social Work Subject Centre (SWAP) 2009).

Managing your pathway

It is really important to take on board that continuing professional development and post-registration training and learning are not necessarily about 'going away' to do a course of study provided by an academic institution. The three 'modes' above emphasise that learning can take place as a result of almost anything that you do, in a wide variety of settings, situations and circumstances, and the trick is to remain alive to what influences your practice and to record the changes you make or the ideas that are consolidated and strengthened, as part of your normal routine, integrated into your everyday practice. This is where a reflexive journal (see Chapter 3) really comes into its own. Adopting this approach should also help you to discover positive connections between your own practice, that of the team, and the culture and strategies of the organisation.

Your line manager must be directly involved in almost every aspect of your professional development, from informal discussion to integration into formal supervision, appraisal and performance systems, so that your individual aspirations are part of a structured plan which coordinates development activities across the needs of the whole team. Links to the wider team and forward planning are more important than you might think. For example, as child care teams, particularly in local authority settings, are frequently under-strength, the support of colleagues is vital. Where your absence is not supported by your colleagues, you may inadvertently lay yourself open to resentment if others are expected to cover your duties when you are perceived to be 'away on a jolly'. We found in our own study that there was a sense in which people often undertook training as a welcome respite from the normal office pressures and workload, but it can backfire if the proper cover arrangements have not been considered, agreed and confirmed to you by your line manager *before* you start your course, as one newly qualified social worker quickly discovered.

> " But in doing the training, there's the other part of you that's worrying because all your work is building up. You know, when you come back off a week's course, there's 150 emails and everything has kicked off and everything is a concern ... well, you're working later every night that week just to unravel it all. (NQSW) "

Another aspect of training that can turn a potentially positive experience into a very negative one is lack of planning to meet the additional personal burdens of study on top of what is probably already a busy and sometimes stressful job. However generous your employer's arrangements are, it is unrealistic to believe that everything can be achieved in your normal contract hours. Your professional development will certainly demand some of your personal time, and you need to have considered all of the implications and made a realistic assessment of how you will manage the extra demands. Comments from two social workers undertaking their first PQ module emphasise this point.

> " Well yes, I did get my study day but there's an awful lot of work that needs to be done outside of that day.
>
> You have to do it in some of your own time ... I spent two complete weekends in addition to my study days, you know where I was saying to my family 'Leave me alone! I need to get this assignment finished.'
>
> (Social workers) "

Table 12.2 Variations in PQ framework requirements in the four UK countries

	England	Northern Ireland	Scotland	Wales
Governance	Care Standards Act 2000	Health and Personal Social Services (NI) Act 2001	Regulation of Care (Scotland) Act 2001	Care Standards Act 2000
Rules	GSCC Approval of Post-Qualifying Course Rules 2005	Rules for the Approval of PQ Education and Training in Social Work, NI	Rules and Requirements for Specialist Training for Social Service Workers in Scotland 2005	Rules approved by National Assembly for Wales, March 2007
Requirements and guidance documentation	Post-qualifying framework for social work education and training (2005)	Northern Ireland Post Qualifying Education and Training Framework in Social Work (2006)	Continuous Learning Framework (CLF) (December 2008)	Module Framework for PQ Learning and Development in Social Work (2005)
What form do the new arrangements for PQ take?	Universities/colleges, approved by GSCC to do so, develop and deliver PQ courses in partnership with employers and stakeholders through Regional Planning Networks	Arrangements are currently under review	Employer-led continuum based on the 4 Scottish Social Services Learning Networks which provide a forum for employer and stakeholders to identify shared learning needs and solutions	CCTW approves programmes under the general Rules above. Programmes must be developed and delivered through a partnership of universities/colleges, employers and service users and carers
What academic level has been set?	Specialist – hons. degree or graduate diploma Higher specialist – postgraduate diploma/master's level Advanced – minimum master's level	The entire framework is at master's level	Specialist training will be available at master's level SCQF 7–11	All programmes will comprise modules capable of being built into qualifications at graduate level (Levels 6 or 7)

Table 12.2 Variations in PQ framework requirements in the four UK countries (continued)

	England	Northern Ireland	Scotland	Wales
Is there a module for the consolidation of practice?	Yes. Consolidation must be demonstrated against generic and specific award requirements as a first module at specialist level	No. This should be covered during the Assessed Year in Employment (AYE) before candidates enter the NI PQ framework. After AYE, candidates can enrol for an Initial Professional Development Programme or similar training provided by employers	There is a range of programmes for this purpose, including child protection	Some universities/colleges are developing modules for consolidation but there are no specific requirements
Can other professions access the framework?	Yes but this does not provide access to a professional award in social work	Enrolment for a PQ award is restricted to registered social workers. Social workers attending multidisciplinary programmes can use those to obtain a PQ award	Continuous Learning Framework applies to the entire social service workforce, although other professions will receive an award with a different title	Yes, in some circumstances but only registered social workers can be awarded a Post Qualifying Award in Social Work
What standards will awards be based on?	National occupational standards underpinning all learning outcomes	National, occupational or recognised agency standards	National occupational standards fully integrated into CLF	National occupational standards indicated for each unit level
End of course transcripts	Students must be provided with an annual transcript, recording the learning outcomes achieved	Students must be provided with an annual transcript, recording the learning outcomes achieved for recording on a new database		Students must be provided with a transcript, recording the learning outcomes achieved at the end of a module

Source: adapted from SWAP (2009)

It might also be helpful to have time for background reading and research and generally preparing your workplace before embarking on a particular course. Again, forward planning as part of a coherent pathway, rather than just grabbing whatever is available, should allow you to build this into your timetable.

In our study we found that often there was no clear policy for attending training, and it was left very much to individuals to take the initiative to find out what and when opportunities were available, and how to get access to them. This is not in itself a bad thing, but there is obvious potential for the generation of competition and feelings of unfairness which can quickly divide or undermine a team.

All of these potential difficulties and tensions would be avoided by good coordination of learning and training opportunities by your line manager. However, before leaving this area, it is worth noting that in our own study we found that often managers had been offered little by way of formal PQ training themselves, and therefore had limited understanding of what was involved or what the benefits in terms of new knowledge and skills might be. Given this deficit, although they were happy to 'let people go on training', often there was little acknowledgement of achievement or interest in the experiences of staff, and only scant attention was paid to providing opportunities for staff to try out their new skills, as three comments illustrate.

> **"** But with reference to encouraging their own personal development plan, well you know, it's more about people just rushing off to do it if and when they have to. (Line manager)
>
> I think a lot of managers see it [PQ study] as just another hurdle. They see it as another thing that is impinging on their workers' time. (NQSW)
>
> And I gave my manager a copy of my portfolio and a few months later I asked him have you read it and he said, 'No, it's in my drawer. I feel awful but I just haven't had time.' (Social worker) **"**

If you find yourself in an agency which does not yet fully embrace a learning culture, you will need to take a proactive stance to ensure that you initiate discussion of PDPs, PQ and PRTL at every appropriate opportunity, both individually and in tandem with team members, so that CPD remains high on the joint agenda.

Progression

In academic terms, progression is frequently thought about as an ascending ladder, with each level building on the one below. In professional development, however, it is helpful to view progression in three dimensions rather than two, like a climbing frame rather than a ladder, with development occurring both horizontally and vertically (e.g. in new settings, tasks and roles, or in greater complexity in a specialist context).

As we write this book, social work education and training, in England at least, is again undergoing fundamental review and change following Lord Laming's (2009) report in the wake of the death of Baby Peter in Haringey and the review being undertaken by the Social Work Taskforce. Although it might be tempting to put CPD on the back burner against this uncertain background, it is not a sensible option. The national occupational standards relevant to specific areas of practice remain a unifying feature of professional development, and you should be able to identify those that are most relevant to your particular area of work in discussion with your manager or agency training and staff development unit. The occupational standards most relevant to your own area of practice should provide you with a firm foundation on which to base your own progression pathway, while still being adaptable enough to be transferred into any new frameworks that might emerge.

Similarly subject to change, promotion within the profession has traditionally taken social workers away from practice into management or education roles. Satisfaction for many social workers is closely linked to their ability to have face-to-face contact with service users, and the lack of opportunity for advancement while staying in contact with direct practice has been noted as a key factor in the recruitment and retention crisis that continues to have a damaging impact on many social work teams, especially in local authorities. As part of a wider strategy to address the difficulties, reflecting the structures already available to the teaching profession, the CWDC in England is currently developing career grades, including that of 'advanced practitioner' status. An active engagement with CPD activities will put you in the best position to move forward as soon as any new career 'route map' emerges.

Presenting your evidence

Whether you are collecting evidence for PRTL, for PQ, for your PDP or for a reflexive journal, there are two aspects of professional development – critical analysis and reflection – that should underpin your thinking and are essential for any written work at post-qualifying level.

CRITICAL ANALYSIS

One of the most important requirements of any work at post-qualifying level is evidence that you can go beyond providing a straightforward chronological description of events, or presentation of information about a subject, simply by organising and rephrasing what other people have written. Critical analysis requires a more significant engagement with the material. You will be attempting to link different ideas and findings together in a logical and persuasive way, and to provide some personal judgement or appraisal of the issues being discussed, commenting on the strengths and weaknesses of the evidence available and the applicability of various theories or models of practice to different circumstances.

There are a number of questions that you may need to ask yourself, in order to develop a critically analytical approach to your material. For example, is the information you are gathering from published sources reliable, being based on well-designed quantitative or qualitative research studies, with large representative samples of respondents? Are the findings from one study applicable to other contexts, times or situations? Is most of the evidence, from a range of different sources, pointing in a similar direction, or are there contradictory findings or significant gaps in our knowledge? How useful is the information available to you as a practitioner in helping you to form judgements about how to act in individual cases? And, in relation to your own practice material, you might be asking yourself, what is actually going on in this family, and why do you think it is happening? In other words, what is your analysis of the factors that are most important in determining the way that particular individuals or groups are behaving?

You will need to demonstrate that you can evaluate the importance that can be attached to the findings of different research studies or the conclusions of official reports and inquiries. Questions such as *who* funded the study, or *how* an inquiry was conducted, and *what* is being claimed in the conclusions, all need to be examined and tested. Just because someone's work appears in print, it should not be accepted uncritically: all material is not of equal value or utility for your work, and you will be expected to comment on these matters. If you think that particular approaches to social work practice, or a set of theoretical ideas, or the findings of certain research studies or inquiry reports are especially important, you need to explain why you have formed that judgement. Similarly, if you find the organisational procedures, government performance targets and social policies, or the latest fashion in social work, to be unhelpful to your practice or the people you are working with, you need to say why you have formed this view.

Furthermore, if you are basing aspects of your analysis on your own experience, you will also need to think critically about how extensive and relevant that experience is. Are your judgements significantly influenced by your own particular beliefs or life experiences and, if they are, in what ways? How likely do you think it is that other workers, dealing with a similar scenario, would come to the same conclusions as you have done? Have you been able to use supervision sessions, or discussions with your colleagues, to check this out? This questioning is an essential ingredient of working at post-qualifying level.

REFLECTION

The other essential element of practice at post-qualifying level considered here is evidence of your capacity for reflection – expressing your thoughts about the impact of your professional practice on yourself and vice versa. One aspect of this, for example, might be a consideration of what you have learned from a particular life experience, or a recent piece of practice that you have undertaken. This could lead on to some thoughts about the ways that these events are likely to influence your practice in the future, or some areas of knowledge or skills you may want to develop further.

In writing about your practice, you will therefore need to record not only what actually happened, but also what you were thinking about what took place, both at the time it happened and afterwards. What emotional impact is your work having upon you and how does your emotional state feed back into the way that you do your job? How well do you think you prepared for, or implemented, a particular piece of work and what, in the light of the outcomes, might you want to do differently in the future? Are any of the barriers to effective practice that you might have identified located within yourself, or are they the product of, say, organisational or legislative factors? This is an opportunity for you to take a step back from the day-to-day engagement with your work, consciously stopping to think about what you are doing and why you are doing it in that way. Have your personal or professional values been challenged or compromised by the nature of the tasks you have been required to undertake, or the wider context within which your work is taking place?

Casting a critical eye over your practice in this way is an important component of your continuing development as a professional child care social worker. It *should* already be a central element in the organisational arrangements provided for the supervision of your work. However, it may have been squeezed out by time pressures, or more procedural, managerial or bureaucratic approaches to social work. Alternatively, you may have been suppressing the process of self-reflection as a personal coping strategy, finding that thinking about your work sometimes is too stressful or painful. None of these reasons for limiting reflections on your practice and experience should be allowed to continue unresolved. Your own personal and professional development, and the services that are provided to vulnerable and disadvantaged people, depend on effective processes for encouraging and supporting the capacity to think reflectively about your work.

Key considerations for successful continuing professional development

- Your continuing professional development and post-registration training and learning are likely to be most successful where you set clear and achievable goals (agreed with your supervisor) within your personal development plan.

- Remember that your continuing professional development can be based on almost anything that you do, including informal learning and day-to-day practice developments, as well as learning through training courses and higher education modules and programmes.

- Keeping a reflexive journal, that incorporates both critical analysis and reflection on your experiences as a newly qualified social worker, will help you to make the links between your own developing practice, that of your colleagues, and the culture and strategies of your employing organisation.

References

Ahearn, K.K., Ferris, G.R., Hochwarter, W.A., Douglas, C. and Ammeter, A.P. (2004) 'Leader political skill and team performance.' *Journal of Management 30*, 3, 309–327.

Association of Directors for Social Services (ADSS) (2005) *Social Work in Wales: A Profession to Value.* Cardiff: ADSS Cymru.

Banks, S. (2002) 'Professional Values and Accountabilities.' In R. Adams, L. Dominelli and M. Payne (eds) *Critical Practice in Social Work.* Basingstoke: Palgrave Macmillan.

Barclay, P. (1982) *Social Workers: Their Role and Tasks (Barclay Report).* London: Bedford Square Press.

Barnett, R. (1997) *Higher Education: A Critical Business.* Buckingham: Open University Press.

Bednar, S.G. (2003) 'Elements of satisfying organisational climates in child welfare agencies.' *Families in Society 84*, 7–12.

Belbin, R.M. (2004) *Management Teams: Why They Succeed or Fail,* 2nd edn. Oxford: Butterworth-Heinemann.

Bennett, P., Evans, R. and Tattersall, A. (1993) 'Stress and coping in social workers: A preliminary investigation.' *British Journal of Social Work 23*, 1, 31–44.

Berkowitz, A.D. and Perkins, H.W. (1984) 'Stress among farm women: Work and family as interacting systems.' *Journal of Marriage and the Family 46*, 1, 161–166.

Brown, A. and Bourne, I. (1996) *The Social Work Supervisor.* Buckingham: Open University Press.

Burton, N.W. and Turrell, G. (2000) 'Occupation, hours worked and leisure-time physical activity.' *Preventative Medicine 31*, 673–681.

Carroll, M. and Gilbert, M.C. (2005) *On Being a Supervisee: Creating Learning Partnerships.* London: Vukani.

Charles, M. and Butler, S. (2004) 'Social Workers' Management of Organisational Change.' In M. Lymbery and S. Butler (eds) *Social Work Ideals and Practice Realities.* Basingstoke: Palgrave Macmillan.

Children's Workforce Development Council (CWDC) (2006) *Continuing Professional Development Strategy for Social Care: Executive Summary.* Leeds: CWDC.

Children's Workforce Development Council (CWDC) (2008a) *Newly-Qualified Social Worker Pilot Programme 2008–2009: NQSW Programme Design.* Leeds: CWDC.

Children's Workforce Development Council (CWDC) (2008b) *Newly-Qualified Social Worker Pilot Programme 2008–2009: Handbook for NQSWs.* Leeds: CWDC.

Clarke, M. and Stewart, J. (1997) *Handling the Wicked Issues: A Challenge for Government.* Birmingham: School of Public Policy, University of Birmingham.

Collins, S. (2007) 'Social workers, resilience, positive emotions and optimism.' *Practice 19*, 4, 255–269.

Collins, S. (2008) 'Statutory social workers: Stress, job satisfaction, coping, social support and individual differences.' *British Journal of Social Work 38*, 6, 1173–1193.

Commission for Social Care Inspection (CSCI) (2006) *Supporting Parents, Safeguarding Children: Meeting the Needs of Parents with Children on the Child Protection Register.* London: CSCI.

Community Care (2005) 'Profession becoming less focused on clients and more on paperwork.' *Community Care*, 15 December.

Community Care (2008) 'GSCC's Mike Wardle calls for minimum client/worker ratio.' *Community Care*, 9 December.

Cooper, B. (2008) 'Continuing Professional Development: A Critical Approach.' In S. Fraser and S. Matthews (eds) *The Critical Practitioner in Health and Social Care*. Milton Keynes: Open University and Sage.

Corbett, D. (1991) *Public Sector Management*. Sydney: Allen and Unwin.

Department for Children, Schools and Families (DCSF) (2009) 'Multi-agency services: Toolkit for practitioners.' *Every Child Matters: Change for Children*. Available at www.dcsf.gov.uk/everychildmatters/strategy/deliveringservices1/multiagencyworking/managerstoolkit/practitionerstoolkit, accessed on 16 June 2009.

Department for Education and Skills (DfES) (2003) *Raising Standards and Tackling Workload: A National Agreement. Time for Standards*. London: Teacher Development Agency and DfES.

Department for Education and Skills (DfES) (2006) *Integrated Children's System: A Statement of Business Requirements*. London: DfES.

Department for Innovation, Universities and Skills (DIUS) (2008) *Lifelong Learning: Developing Our Brains from Cradle to Grave. Foresight Report*. London: DIUS. Available at www.lifelonglearning.co.uk/ln08112.htm, accessed on 26 May 2009.

Department of Health (2002) *Requirements for Social Work Training*. London: Department of Health.

Department of Health (2006) *Options for Excellence: Building the Social Care Workforce of the Future*. London: Department of Health.

Dreyfus, H. and Dreyfus, S. (1986) *Mind Over Machine: The Power of Human Intuition and Expertise in the Era of the Computer*. Oxford: Basil Blackwell.

Eraut, M. (1994) *Developing Professional Knowledge and Competence*. London: Falmer.

Fineman, S. (1985) *Social Work Stress and Intervention*. Aldershot: Gower.

Fink, S.C., Beak, J. and Taddeo, K. (1971) 'Organizational crisis and change.' *Journal of Applied Behavioural Science 17*, 1, 14–37.

Fook, J. and Gardner, F. (2007) *Practising Critical Reflection*. Maidenhead: Open University Press.

Fook, J., Ryan, M. and Hawkins, L. (2000) *Professional Expertise: Practice, Theory and Education for Working in Uncertainty*. London: Whiting and Birch.

French, R. (2001) '"Negative capability": Managing the confusing uncertainties of change.' *Journal of Organizational Change Management 14*, 5, 480–492.

General Social Care Council (GSCC) (2002) *Codes of Practice for Social Care Workers and Employers*. London: GSCC.

General Social Care Council (GSCC) (2006a) *Post-Qualifying Framework for Social Work Education and Training*. London: GSCC.

General Social Care Council (GSCC) (2006b) *Post Registration Training and Learning (PRTL) Requirements for Registered Social Workers: Advice and Guidance on Good Practice*. London: GSCC. Available at www.gscc.org.uk/NR/rdonlyres/A9B67C8C-329C-4EED-97A9-2423BD3B1D91/0/PRTLGUIDANCEFINAL May2006.pdf, accessed on 26 May 2009.

General Social Care Council (GSCC) (2008a) *Raising Standards: Social Work Conduct in England 2003–08*. London: GSCC.

General Social Care Council (GSCC) (2008b) *Social Work at its Best: A Statement of Social Work Roles and Tasks for the 21st Century*. London: GSCC.

Gerrish, K. (2005) 'Still fumbling along? A comparative study of newly-qualified nurses' perception of the transition from student to qualified nurse.' *Journal of Advanced Nursing 32*, 2, 473–480.

Glisson, C. and Hemmelgarn, A. (1998) 'The effects of organisational climate and inter-organizational coordination on the quality and outcomes of children's service systems.' *Child Abuse and Neglect 22*, 5, 401–421.

Gordon, R. and Hendry, E. (2001) 'Supervising Assessments of Children and Families: The Role of the Front Line Manager.' In J. Horwath (ed.) *The Child's World: Assessing Children in Need.* London: Jessica Kingsley Publishers.

Gould, N. (2000) 'Becoming a learning organisation: A social work example.' *Social Work Education 19*, 6, 585–596.

Gould, N. and Baldwin, M. (2004) *Social Work, Critical Reflection and the Learning Organisation.* Aldershot, UK: Ashgate.

Handy, C. (1993) *Understanding Organisations.* Harmondsworth: Penguin.

Harrison, R. (1972) 'Understanding your organization's character.' *Harvard Business Review 50*, 3, 119–128.

Hawkins, P. and Shohet, R. (2006) *Supervision in the Helping Professions*, 3rd edn. Buckingham: Open University Press.

Heron, J. (1975) *Six-Category Intervention Analysis.* Guildford: Human Potential Research Project, University of Surrey.

Hughes, L. and Pengelly, P. (1997) *Staff Supervision in a Turbulent Environment: Managing Process and Task in Front-line Services.* London: Jessica Kingsley Publishers.

Hughes, M. and Wearing, M. (2007) *Organisations and Management in Social Work.* London: Sage.

Jack, G. (1997) 'An ecological approach to social work with children and families.' *Child and Family Social Work 2*, 2, 109–120.

Jenaro, C., Flores, N. and Arias, B. (2007) 'Burnout and coping in human service practitioners.' *Professional Psychology: Research and Practice 38*, 1, 80–87.

Jimmieson, N.L. (2000) 'Employee reactions to behavioural control under conditions of stress: The moderating role of self-efficacy.' *Work and Stress 14*, 3, 262–280.

Johns, C. (1994) 'Guided Reflection.' In A. Palmer, S. Burns and C. Bulman (eds) *Reflective Practice in Nursing.* Chichester: Blackwell Scientific Publishers.

Jones, C. (2001) 'Voices from the front line: State social workers and New Labour.' *British Journal of Social Work 31*, 547–562.

Jones, F., Fletcher, B.E.N. and Ibbetson, K. (1991) 'Stressors and strains among social workers: Demands, supports, constraints, and psychological health.' *British Journal of Social Work 21*, 5, 443–469.

Kadushin, A. (1976) *Supervision in Social Work.* New York: Columbia University Press.

Kadushin, A. (1985) *Supervision in Social Work*, 2nd edn. New York: Columbia University Press.

Karasek, R.A. (1979) 'Job demands, job decision, latitude and mental strain: Implications for job redesign.' *Administrative Science Quarterly 24*, 285–308.

Kirschbaum, C., Klauer, T., Filipp, S.H. and Hellhammer, D.H. (1995) 'Sex-specific effects of social support on cortisol and subjective responses to acute psychological stress.' *Psychosomatic Medicine 57*, 1, 23–31.

Kolb, D. (1984) *Experiential Learning.* Englewood Cliffs, NJ: Prentice Hall.

Kouvonen, A., Kivimäki, M., Elovainio, M., Virtanen, M., Linna, A. and Vahtera, J. (2005) 'Job strain and leisure-time physical activity in female and male public sector employees.' *Preventive Medicine 41*, 2, 532–539.

Kramer, M. (1974) *Reality Shock: Why Nurses Leave Nursing.* St Louis, MO: CV Mosby.

Lacey, C. (1977) *The Socialisation of Teachers.* London: Methuen.

Laming, W.H. (2003) *Report of the Enquiry into the Death of Victoria Climbié.* London: The Stationery Office.

Laming, W.H. (2009) *The Protection of Children in England: A Progress Report.* London: The Stationery Office.

Lazarus, R.S. and Folkman, S. (1984) *Stress, Appraisal and Coping.* New York: Springer.

Lens, V. (2004) 'Principled negotiation: A new tool for case advocacy.' *Social Work 49*, 3, 506–513.

Lepore, S.J., Ragan, J.D. and Jones, S. (2000) 'Talking facilitates cognitive emotional processes of adaptation to an acute stressor.' *Journal of Personality and Social Psychology 78*, 3, 499–508.

Lewin, K. (1952) *Field Theory in Social Science.* New York: Harper and Row.

Lick, D.W. (2006) 'A new perspective on organizational learning: Creating learning teams.' *Evaluation and Program Planning 29*, 1, 88–96.

Lysons, K. (1997) 'Organisational analysis.' *British Journal of Administrative Management 18*, March–April (supplement).

Maben, J. and Macleod Clark, J. (1998) 'Project 2000 diplomates' perceptions of experiences of transition from student to staff nurse.' *Journal of Clinical Nursing 7*, 145–153.

McGee, R.A. (1989) 'Burnout and professional decision making: An analogue study.' *Journal of Counseling Psychology 36*, 3, 345–351.

McLenachan, J. (2006) 'Facing up to a recruitment crisis.' *Guardian*, 27 November. Available at www.guardian.co.uk/society/2006/nov/27/socialcare.comment, accessed on 26 May 2009.

Martin, R.A. (2001) 'Humor, laughter, and physical health: Methodological issues and research findings.' *Psychological Bulletin 127*, 4, 504–519.

Maslach, C. (1980) *Burnout: The Cost of Caring*. Englewood Cliffs, NJ: Prentice Hall.

Maslach, C. and Leiter, M.P. (1997) *The Truth about Burnout: How Organisations Cause Personal Stress and What to Do About It*. San Francisco, CA: Jossey-Bass.

Maslow, A.H. (1943) 'A theory of human motivation.' *Psychological Review 50*, 370–396.

Mattinson, J. (1981) 'The deadly equal triangle.' In *Change and Renewal in Psychodynamic Social Work: British and American Developments in Practice and Education for Services in Families and Children*. Northampton, MA: School of Social Work, Smith College.

Michie, S. and Cockcroft, A. (1996) 'Overwork can kill.' *British Medical Journal 312*, 921–922.

Middleman, R. and Rhodes, G. (1980) 'Teaching the practice of supervision.' *Journal of Education for Social Work 16*, 51–59.

Mooney, M. (2007) 'Newly-qualified Irish nurses' interpretation of their preparation and experiences of registration.' *Journal of Clinical Nursing 15*, 1610–1617.

Moran, C.C. and Hughes, L.P. (2006) 'Coping with stress: Social work students and humour.' *Social Work Education 25*, 5, 501–517.

Morgan, R. (2006) *About Social Workers: A Children's Views Report*. Newcastle: Commission for Social Care Inspectorate.

Morris, L. (2005) 'The process of decision-making by stressed social workers: To stay or leave the workplace.' *International Review of Psychiatry 17*, 5, 347–354.

Morrison, T. (2001) *Staff Supervision in Social Care: Making a Real Difference for Staff and Service Users*. Brighton: Pavilion.

Nellis, M. (2001) 'The diploma in probation studies in the Midland region: Celebration and critique after the first two years.' *Howard Journal 40*, 4, 377–401.

Noakes, S., Hearn, B., Burton, S. and Wonnacott, J. (1998) *Developing Good Child Protection Practice: A Guide for First Line Managers*. London: National Children's Bureau.

Parkinson, J. and Pritchard, J. (2005) 'The induction experiences of newly-qualified secondary teachers in England and Wales.' *Journal of In-Service Education 31*, 1, 63–81.

Pearson, G. (1973) 'Social work as the privatized solution of public ills.' *British Journal of Social Work 3*, 2, 209–227.

Plant, R. (1987) *Managing Change and Making It Stick*. London: Fontana.

Platt, D. (2007) *The Status of Social Care: A Review 2007*. London: Department of Health.

Pont, C. (2000) 'Assessment summary of findings of child care inspections 1992–97.' In Department of Health, *Studies Informing the Framework for the Assessment of Children in Need and their Families*. Norwich: The Stationery Office.

Rauktis, M.E. and Koeske, G.F. (1994) 'Maintaining social worker morale: When supportive supervision is not enough.' *Administration in Social Work 18*, 1, 39–60.

Roberts, A.R. (2000) *Crisis Intervention Handbook: Assessment, Treatment and Research*, 2nd edn. Oxford: Oxford University Press.

Robinson, V. (1936) *Supervision in Social Casework: A Problem in Professional Education*. Chapel Hill, NC: University of North Carolina Press.

Rogers, A.M. (2001) 'Nurture, bureaucracy and re-balancing the mind and heart.' *Journal of Social Work Practice 15*, 2, 181–191.

Royal College of Nursing (RCN) (1999) *Look Back, Move On: Clinical Supervision for Nurses*. London: RCN.

Sargent, L.D. and Terry, D.J. (2000) 'The moderating role of social support in Karasek's job strain model.' *Work and Stress 14*, 3, 245–261.

Schön, D. (1983) *The Reflective Practitioner*. New York: Basic Books.

Scottish Executive (2002) *Action Plan for the Social Services Workforce*. Edinburgh: Scottish Executive.

Scottish Executive (2006) *Changing Lives: Report of the 21st Century Social Work Review*. Edinburgh: Scottish Executive.

Seebohm, F. (1968) *Report of the Committee on Local Authority and Allied Personal Social Services (Seebohm Report)*. London: HMSO.

Seligman, M. (1975) *Learned Helplessness*. San Francisco, CA: Freeman.

Seligman, M. (2006) *Learned Optimism: How to Change Your Mind and Your Life*. New York: Vintage.

Shulman, L. (1982) *Skills of Supervision and Staff Management*. Itasca, IL: F.E. Peacock.

Siviter, B. (2008) *The Newly-Qualified Nurse's Handbook: A Survival Guide*. Edinburgh: Baillière Tindall.

Skills for Care (2008) *What Leaders and Managers in Adult Social Care Do: A Statement for a Leadership and Management Development Strategy for Social Care*. Leeds: Skills for Care.

Smith, M. and Nursten, J. (1998) 'Social workers' experience of distress: Moving towards change?' *British Journal of Social Work 28*, 3, 351–368.

Social Care Institute for Excellence (SCIE) (2004) *Learning Organisations: A Self-Assessment Resource Pack – Key Characteristics*. Available at www.scie.org.uk/publications/learningorgs/files/key_characteristics_2.pdf, accessed on 26 May 2009.

Social Care Workforce Research Unit (SCWRU) (2008) *Evaluation of the New Social Work Degree Qualification in England. Volume 1: Findings*. London: Social Care Workforce Research Unit, King's College London.

Social Policy and Social Work Subject Centre (SWAP) (2009) 'Matrix showing the variations of requirements for the post-qualifying education and training in social work for the four UK countries.' Available at www.swap.ac.uk/docs/pq_uk_matrix_collated_jan09.pdf, accessed on 26 May 2009.

Stalker, C.A., Mandell, D., Frensch, J.M., Harvey, C. and Wright, M. (2007) 'Child welfare workers who are exhausted yet satisfied with their jobs: How do they do it?' *Child and Family Social Work 12*, 182–191.

Statham, J., Cameron, C. and Mooney, A. (2006) *The Tasks and Roles of Social Workers: A Focused Overview of Research Evidence*. London: Thomas Coram Research Institute.

Stevenson, O. (1981) *Specialisation in Social Service Teams*. London: Allen and Unwin.

Storey, J. and Billingham, J. (2001) 'Occupational stress and social work.' *Social Work Education 20*, 6, 659–670.

Tadeka, F., Ibaraki, N., Yokoyama, E., Miyake, T. and Ohida, T. (2005) 'The relationship of job type to burnout in social workers at social welfare offices.' *Journal of Occupational Therapy 47*, 119–125.

Taylor, S.E., Klein, L.C., Lewis, B.P., Gruenewald, T.L., Gurung, R.A.R. and Updegraff, J.A. (2000) 'Biobehavioral responses to stress in females: Tend-and-befriend, not fight-or-flight.' *Psychological Review 107*, 3, 411–429.

Thody, A., Gray, B. and Bowden, D. (2000) *The Teacher's Survival Guide*. London: Continuum.

Thompson, N., Stradling, S., Murphy, M. and O'Neill, P. (1996) 'Stress and organizational culture.' *British Journal of Social Work 26*, 5, 647–665.

Tickle, L. (1994) *The Induction of New Teachers: Reflective Professional Practice*. London: Cassell.

TOPSS UK Partnership (2002) *The National Occupational Standards for Social Work*. Leeds: Topss/Skills for Care.

Trades Union Congress (TUC) (2006) *Biennial Safety Survey of Representatives*, 30 October. Available at www.tuc.org.uk/h_and_s/tuc-12579-f0.cfm, accessed on 26 May 2009.

Tuckman, B.W. (1965) 'Developmental sequence in small groups.' *Psychological Bulletin 63*, 6, 384–399.

UNISON (2008) *UNISON's 10-Point Plan for Protecting Vulnerable Children*. Available at www.unison.org.uk/acrobat/18035.pdf, accessed on 26 May 2009.

Warren, C. (1993) *Family Centres and the Children Act 1989*. Arundel, UK: Tarrant.

Welsh Assembly Government (2007) *A Strategy for Social Services in Wales over the Next Decade: Fulfilled Lives, Supportive Communities*. Cardiff: Welsh Assembly Government.

Wharton, A.S. and Erickson, R.J. (1995) 'The consequences of caring: Exploring the links between women's job and family emotional work.' *Sociological Quarterly 36*, 273–296.

Wikipedia (2001) 'Presenteeism: Dr. Cary Cooper.' Available at http://en.wikipedia.org/wiki/Presenteeism, accessed on 26 May 2009.

Wrzesniewski, A. and Dutton, J.E. (2001) 'Crafting a job: Revisioning employees as active crafters of their work.' *Academy of Management Review 26*, 179–201.

Yelloly, M. and Henkel, M. (eds) (1995) *Learning and Teaching in Social Work: Towards Reflective Practice*. London: Jessica Kingsley Publishers.

Ying, Y.-W. (2008) 'The buffering effect of self-detachment against emotional exhaustion among social work students.' *Journal of Religion and Spirituality in Social Work: Social Thought 27*, 1, 127–146.

Subject Index